A Hillbilly Elegy for America

A Hillbilly Elegy for America:

J.D. Vance and What His Partnership with Trump Means for the Nation

D. E. Sargent

Table of Contents

Introduction

In 2024, the American political landscape is at a pivotal juncture. The nation stands divided, grappling with issues that span economic disparity, healthcare crises, and cultural shifts. Amidst this backdrop, a new political partnership has emerged—one that promises to reshape the future of this nation. Enter J.D. Vance and Donald Trump, a duo that brings together a blend of fresh perspectives and seasoned leadership.

You might be wondering, why Vance? And why now? Well, folks, this isn't just another political pairing—this is a strategic alliance poised to bring real, tangible change to America's working class and address some of the most pressing issues of our time, like the opioid crisis. This partnership is not about empty promises or political posturing; it's about actionable plans and real solutions.

Donald Trump, a name that needs no introduction, has always been a figure of relentless energy and unyielding determination. His presidency was marked by bold decisions and unorthodox approaches that left an indelible mark on American politics. From his hardline stance on immigration to his aggressive trade policies, Trump's tenure was characterized by a commitment to shaking up the status quo and putting America first. Now, in 2024, Trump has chosen to step back into the arena, but this time with a new running mate who embodies a fresh perspective and a connection to the very heart of America's working class—J.D. Vance.

J.D. Vance, a man whose life story reads like a modern-day epic, has risen from the depths of poverty and adversity to become a beacon of hope for many Americans. His journey from the troubled streets of Middletown, Ohio, to the hallowed halls of Yale Law School, and now to the forefront of American politics, is nothing short of extraordinary. Vance's life is a testament to the power of resilience, determination, and the unwavering belief in the American Dream.

This book will take you on a journey through their plans, their policies, and their vision for the future. But first, let's get to know the man at the center of it all: J.D. Vance.

The Trump-Vance Partnership: A Strategic Alliance

The announcement of J.D. Vance as Donald Trump's running mate for the 2024 election took many by surprise. On the surface, their backgrounds couldn't be more different—Trump, the billionaire real estate mogul turned president, and Vance, the self-made author and politician who pulled himself up by his bootstraps. Yet, beneath these differences lies a shared vision and a common goal: to revitalize America and restore the promise of the American Dream for all citizens.

Their partnership represents a strategic alliance that combines Trump's experience and charisma with Vance's fresh perspective and deep connection to the working class. Together, they form a political force that is both dynamic and formidable, capable of addressing the multifaceted challenges facing the nation today.

Trump: The Seasoned Leader

Donald Trump's impact on American politics is undeniable. His presidency from 2016 to 2020 was a period marked by significant upheaval and change. Trump's approach was anything but conventional, and his policies often sparked intense debate and controversy. Yet, his ability to connect with a broad swath of the American electorate, particularly those who felt left behind by the political establishment, was unparalleled.

During his presidency, Trump focused on key issues such as immigration reform, economic growth, and national security. His administration implemented tax cuts that were touted as a boon for American businesses and workers alike. Trump also renegotiated trade deals to prioritize American interests, withdrew the United States from international agreements he deemed unfavorable, and took a hard stance on illegal immigration.

Despite facing significant opposition and criticism, Trump's presidency energized a base of supporters who believed in his vision of putting America first. His ability to galvanize this support and create a movement that transcended traditional party lines is a testament to his political acumen and leadership skills.

Vance: The Fresh Perspective

J.D. Vance's journey to the political arena is a story of perseverance and determination. Born into a working-class family in Middletown, Ohio, Vance's early life was marked by hardship and instability. His mother's struggle with addiction and the economic challenges facing his community shaped his worldview and instilled in him a deep empathy for those who face similar struggles.

Vance's memoir, "Hillbilly Elegy," chronicles his life story and offers a candid look at the challenges facing the white working class in America. The book became a bestseller and a cultural phenomenon, resonating with readers across the political spectrum. Through his writing, Vance articulated the frustrations and hopes of a segment of the population that often feels overlooked and marginalized.

After serving in the Marine Corps and attending Yale Law School, Vance turned his attention to politics. His experiences gave him a unique perspective on the socio-economic issues facing the nation, and he became a vocal advocate for policies aimed at revitalizing the American Dream. Vance's political career has been characterized by his commitment to addressing the opioid crisis, supporting economic policies that benefit the working class, and enhancing healthcare access in rural areas.

A Vision for America

The Trump-Vance ticket for 2024 is built on a vision of revitalizing America. At the heart of their campaign is a commitment to addressing the economic and social challenges that have left many Americans feeling disenfranchised. Their policies aim to create jobs, support American manufacturing, combat the opioid epidemic, and improve healthcare access.

Economic revitalization is a cornerstone of their platform. Trump and Vance understand that a strong economy is the foundation of a prosperous society. Their policies focus on supporting small businesses, reducing regulatory burdens, and investing in infrastructure projects that create jobs and stimulate economic growth. By prioritizing American manufacturing and ensuring fair trade practices, they aim to bring back jobs that have been lost to globalization and automation.

Combatting the opioid crisis is another critical aspect of their agenda. Vance's personal connection to this issue drives his commitment to finding comprehensive solutions. The opioid epidemic has devastated communities across the nation, and addressing it requires a multifaceted approach that includes prevention, treatment, and support for those affected. Trump and Vance propose policies that increase funding for addiction treatment programs, enhance law enforcement efforts to combat illegal drug trafficking, and support education and prevention initiatives.

Healthcare is another key focus of the Trump-Vance partnership. They recognize that access to quality healthcare is a fundamental need for all Americans, particularly those in rural areas who often face significant barriers to care. Their healthcare proposals aim to improve access, reduce costs, and ensure that rural communities have the resources they need to provide comprehensive care to their residents.

The Road Ahead

The 2024 election is shaping up to be one of the most consequential in recent history. As the nation grapples with economic uncertainty, social unrest, and a lingering pandemic, the choice of leadership will have far-reaching implications for the future. The Trump-Vance ticket offers a vision of hope and renewal, built on the promise of restoring the American Dream and addressing the challenges facing the nation.

In the chapters that follow, we will delve deeper into the lives and careers of J.D. Vance and Donald Trump. We will explore their policies in detail, examine their strategies for the 2024 election, and analyze the potential impact of their administration on America's future. This book will provide you with a comprehensive understanding of their vision and the transformative changes they aim to bring about.

Join us on this journey as we explore the dynamic partnership of J.D. Vance and Donald Trump, and discover how their combined efforts could reshape the future of the United States. This is not just a political campaign—it is a movement for real change, and it is a story that every American needs to hear.

A Hillbilly Elegy for America

Chapter 1: From Humble Beginnings to Political Prominence

J.D. Vance is a name that has become synonymous with resilience and grit. Born in Middletown, Ohio, Vance's early life was anything but easy. His story, as recounted in his best-selling memoir "Hillbilly Elegy," paints a vivid picture of the struggles and triumphs that have shaped him into the man he is today. In this chapter, we will explore Vance's journey from his humble beginnings to his rise in the political arena, examining the key moments and influences that have defined his path.

Early Life and Challenges

J.D. Vance was born James David Vance on August 2, 1984, in Middletown, Ohio, a once-thriving steel town that had fallen on hard times. His early years were marked by the kind of challenges that many Americans can relate to—economic instability, family turmoil, and a community grappling with the effects of deindustrialization. Vance's mother, Bev, struggled with addiction, cycling through relationships and jobs, which created a turbulent home environment for Vance and his sister, Lindsay.

Growing up, Vance faced significant obstacles that could have easily derailed his future. The instability at home, combined with the economic decline of Middletown, painted a bleak picture for many in his community. Yet, through it all, Vance found solace and strength in his grandmother, Bonnie Blanton, whom he affectionately called "Mamaw." Mamaw was a tough, no-nonsense woman who had a profound impact on Vance's life. Her unwavering support and tough love instilled in him a fierce determination to rise above his circumstances.

Mamaw's influence was a guiding light in Vance's life, teaching him the values of hard work, perseverance, and the importance of education.

Despite her own hardships, including a troubled marriage and financial struggles, Mamaw was a pillar of strength for Vance. She made it clear to him that education was the key to escaping the cycle of poverty that had ensnared so many in their community.

Military Service and Academic Achievement

After graduating from Middletown High School, Vance enlisted in the United States Marine Corps, a decision that would prove to be a turning point in his life. The military provided him with structure, discipline, and a sense of purpose that had been lacking in his tumultuous upbringing. Vance served in Iraq as a public affairs specialist, where he learned invaluable lessons in leadership and resilience. His time in the Marines not only shaped his character but also broadened his understanding of the world and the complexities of global politics.

Following his military service, Vance pursued higher education with a newfound determination. He attended Ohio State University, where he excelled academically, graduating summa cum laude with a degree in political science and philosophy. His academic success at Ohio State paved the way for his acceptance into Yale Law School, one of the most prestigious law schools in the country.

At Yale, Vance was exposed to a world far removed from his Appalachian roots. The experience was both enlightening and challenging, as he navigated the cultural and social differences between his upbringing and the elite environment of Yale. Despite the challenges, Vance thrived, earning his Juris Doctor degree and making connections that would later prove invaluable in his career.

The Making of "Hillbilly Elegy"

It was during his time at Yale that Vance began to reflect deeply on his upbringing and the broader socio-economic issues facing communities like Middletown. These reflections culminated in the writing of his memoir, "Hillbilly Elegy: A Memoir of a Family and Culture in Crisis." Published in 2016, the book offers a poignant and candid look at the struggles of the white working-class in America, particularly in the Rust Belt and Appalachian regions.

"Hillbilly Elegy" struck a chord with readers across the political spectrum. Its raw, unflinching portrayal of life in a struggling community resonated with many who saw their own experiences reflected in Vance's story. The book became a national bestseller and catapulted Vance into the national spotlight, establishing him as a prominent voice on issues of poverty, addiction, and social mobility.

Vance's memoir not only brought him fame but also sparked important conversations about the socio-economic challenges facing large swaths of the American population. It highlighted the need for policies that address these issues head-on and underscored the importance of understanding the cultural and historical context of these communities.

Rise to Political Prominence

Vance's foray into politics was driven by a deep-seated desire to give a voice to the voiceless and to advocate for policies that would uplift the working class. His sharp intellect, coupled with his authentic connection to the struggles of everyday Americans, quickly earned him a reputation as a formidable and relatable political figure.

After the success of "Hillbilly Elegy," Vance entered the political arena with a focus on addressing the issues he had written about so passionately. He joined the venture capital firm Mithril Capital, where he gained experience in the business world and continued to build his network of influential contacts. However, his true passion lay in public service, and he soon turned his attention to a career in politics.

In 2021, Vance announced his candidacy for the U.S. Senate from Ohio. His campaign was characterized by a no-nonsense approach and a relentless focus on the issues that mattered most to his constituents. He spoke candidly about the challenges facing the working class and offered practical solutions to address them. His message resonated with voters, and he quickly gained traction as a rising star in the Republican Party.

Key Political Positions and Policies

Vance's political platform is grounded in his commitment to addressing the socio-economic challenges facing America. His key positions and policies reflect his deep understanding of these issues and his dedication to finding effective solutions.

Economic Revitalization: Vance is a staunch advocate for policies that support American manufacturing and create jobs for the working class. He believes in reducing regulatory burdens, investing in infrastructure projects, and ensuring fair trade practices to bring back jobs that have been lost to globalization and automation.

Combating the Opioid Crisis: Having witnessed the devastating impact of the opioid epidemic firsthand, Vance is committed to finding comprehensive solutions to this crisis. His proposals include increasing funding for addiction treatment programs, enhancing law enforcement efforts to combat illegal drug trafficking, and supporting education and prevention initiatives.

Healthcare Access: Vance recognizes that access to quality healthcare is a fundamental need for all Americans, particularly those in rural areas who often face significant barriers to care. His healthcare proposals aim to improve access, reduce costs, and ensure that rural communities have the resources they need to provide comprehensive care to their residents.

Education Reform: Vance is a proponent of education reform that prioritizes vocational training and apprenticeships, ensuring that students are equipped with the skills they need to succeed in the workforce. He also advocates for policies that support school choice and empower parents to make the best decisions for their children's education.

The Trump-Vance Dynamic

The partnership between Trump and Vance is one that blends experience with fresh perspectives. Trump's tenure as President was marked by bold moves and a relentless pursuit of policies aimed at putting America first. His choice of Vance as a running mate signals a continuation of this vision, with a renewed focus on the issues that matter most to everyday Americans.

Vance brings to the table a deep understanding of the challenges facing the working class, informed by his own experiences and his extensive work in the Senate. Together, Trump and Vance represent a powerful force, uniting experience, vision, and a shared commitment to revitalizing the American Dream.

Trump's decision to choose Vance as his running mate was not only strategic but also symbolic. It represents a passing of the torch to a new generation of leaders who are deeply connected to the struggles of everyday Americans. Vance's presence on the ticket adds credibility to Trump's message of economic revitalization and social renewal, making the Trump-Vance partnership a formidable force in the 2024 election.

Vance's Impact and Influence

Since his entry into politics, Vance has made a significant impact on the national stage. His authentic connection to the working class and his willingness to tackle difficult issues head-on have earned him widespread respect and admiration. He has been a vocal advocate for policies that address the root causes of poverty and addiction, and his efforts have already begun to yield positive results.

Vance's influence extends beyond his policy proposals. He has become a symbol of hope and resilience for many Americans who see their own struggles reflected in his story. His ability to articulate the frustrations and aspirations of the working class has made him a powerful voice in American politics.

In addition to his policy work, Vance has also been a prolific commentator and thought leader. He has written numerous op-eds and articles on a wide range of issues, from economic policy to cultural trends. His insights and analysis have been featured in major publications, further cementing his status as a prominent figure in the political landscape.

The Road Ahead

As Vance continues to rise in prominence, the road ahead is filled with both challenges and opportunities. The 2024 election will be a critical moment in his political career, as he and Trump seek to convince the American people that their vision for the future is the right one. The stakes are high, and the outcome of the election will have far-reaching implications for the nation.

Vance's journey from Middletown to the national stage is a testament to the power of perseverance and the enduring promise of the American Dream. His story serves as a reminder that, despite the challenges we face, it is possible to rise above adversity and make a meaningful impact on the world.

In the chapters that follow, we will delve deeper into the lives and careers of J.D. Vance and Donald Trump. We will explore their policies in detail, examine their strategies for the 2024 election, and analyze the potential impact of their administration on America's future. This book will provide you with a comprehensive understanding of their vision and the transformative changes they aim to bring about.

Join us on this journey as we explore the dynamic partnership of J.D. Vance and Donald Trump, and discover how their combined efforts could reshape the future of the United States. This is not just a political campaign—it is a movement for real change, and it is a story that every American needs to hear.

Chapter 2: The Trump-Vance Alliance

The 2024 presidential campaign introduced a dynamic and unexpected alliance between Donald Trump and J.D. Vance. This partnership represents a convergence of experience and fresh perspectives, embodying a strategic blend designed to appeal to a broad spectrum of voters. In this chapter, we will explore how this alliance was formed, the dynamics between Trump and Vance, their shared goals, and the potential implications of their collaboration for the future of American politics.

The Genesis of the Partnership

The partnership between Donald Trump and J.D. Vance was not an overnight development. It was the result of careful consideration, mutual respect, and a shared vision for America's future. To understand how this alliance came to be, it is essential to examine the individual journeys of both men and how their paths intersected.

Donald Trump's entry into politics was marked by his 2016 presidential campaign, which defied all expectations and conventional political wisdom. Trump, a billionaire real estate mogul and reality TV star, leveraged his celebrity status and business acumen to capture the imagination of a significant portion of the American electorate. His campaign focused on themes of economic nationalism, immigration reform, and a promise to "Make America Great Again." Despite facing significant opposition from both the media and the political establishment, Trump secured a decisive victory, becoming the 45th President of the United States.

During his presidency, Trump implemented a series of bold policies aimed at stimulating economic growth, renegotiating trade deals, and reducing regulatory burdens on businesses. His administration was characterized by a mix of controversial decisions and significant accomplishments, including tax cuts, criminal justice reform, and a robust economy prior to the COVID-19 pandemic. However, Trump's presidency was also marked by intense polarization and controversy, culminating in a contested 2020 election and the events of January 6, 2021.

J.D. Vance, on the other hand, came to prominence through his best-selling memoir "Hillbilly Elegy," which chronicled his life growing up in a struggling Rust Belt community. Vance's story resonated with many Americans who felt left behind by economic changes and cultural shifts. His book highlighted the challenges facing the white working class and brought attention to issues such as addiction, poverty, and the decline of traditional industries. Vance's authentic connection to these issues and his thoughtful analysis made him a respected voice in both political and intellectual circles.

Vance's foray into politics was driven by a desire to address the systemic issues he had witnessed firsthand. His candidacy for the U.S. Senate in Ohio was supported by a platform focused on economic revitalization, healthcare reform, and tackling the opioid crisis. Vance's background and policy positions aligned closely with the concerns of many of Trump's supporters, making him a natural ally for the former president.

The initial connection between Trump and Vance was facilitated by mutual acquaintances within conservative circles. Both men shared a common goal of addressing the needs of the working class and revitalizing American manufacturing. Their discussions revealed a shared vision for the future of the country, one that emphasized economic growth, national security, and social stability. This alignment of values and objectives laid the groundwork for a formal partnership.

The Decision to Partner

The decision for Donald Trump to select J.D. Vance as his running mate was strategic and symbolic. Trump's choice was influenced by several factors, including Vance's background, his policy positions, and his ability to connect with voters who felt disenfranchised by the political establishment. Vance's personal story of overcoming adversity resonated with many Americans, making him an appealing figure to complement Trump's established brand.

From a strategic standpoint, Vance brought a fresh perspective and a sense of authenticity to the ticket. His experiences growing up in a struggling community and his subsequent rise to prominence provided a compelling narrative that could attract a wide range of voters. Vance's deep understanding of the issues facing the working class and his commitment to finding practical solutions aligned perfectly with Trump's "America First" agenda.

Trump's decision was also influenced by Vance's potential to broaden the coalition of voters. Vance's appeal extended beyond traditional Republican voters, resonating with independents and even some Democrats who were disillusioned with their party's direction. By choosing Vance, Trump aimed to build a broader, more inclusive coalition that could secure a decisive victory in the 2024 election.

The announcement of the Trump-Vance ticket was met with a mix of surprise and enthusiasm. For many, it represented a bold and innovative move that signaled a commitment to addressing the country's most pressing challenges. The partnership was seen as a powerful combination of experience and new ideas, with the potential to bring about meaningful change.

The Dynamics of the Partnership

The dynamics between Donald Trump and J.D. Vance are characterized by mutual respect and a shared vision for America's future. Despite their different backgrounds and experiences, both men bring complementary strengths to the partnership, creating a synergistic relationship that enhances their collective impact.

Donald Trump, with his years of experience in business and politics, brings a wealth of knowledge and a proven track record of leadership. His ability to command attention, mobilize support, and implement bold policies has been demonstrated throughout his career. Trump's charisma and larger-than-life persona make him a formidable presence on the campaign trail, capable of energizing crowds and galvanizing his base.

J.D. Vance, on the other hand, offers a fresh perspective and a deep understanding of the issues facing everyday Americans. His background in venture capital and his work on addressing social and economic challenges provide him with a unique set of skills and insights. Vance's authenticity and relatability make him an effective communicator, capable of connecting with voters on a personal level.

Together, Trump and Vance form a partnership that balances experience with innovation. Trump's strategic acumen and Vance's thoughtful analysis create a powerful combination that is well-suited to address the complex challenges facing the nation. Their collaboration is built on a foundation of shared values and a commitment to achieving tangible results.

Shared Goals and Objectives

The Trump-Vance partnership is driven by a set of shared goals and objectives that form the core of their campaign platform. These goals reflect their commitment to revitalizing the American Dream and addressing the needs of the working class. Key areas of focus include economic revitalization, healthcare reform, national security, and social stability.

Economic Revitalization: One of the primary goals of the Trump-Vance partnership is to stimulate economic growth and create jobs for the American people. They aim to achieve this by supporting American manufacturing, reducing regulatory burdens, and investing in infrastructure projects. Their economic policies are designed to ensure that the benefits of growth are broadly shared, with a particular focus on revitalizing struggling communities.

Healthcare Reform: Addressing the healthcare needs of the American people is another key objective of the Trump-Vance campaign. They recognize that access to quality healthcare is a fundamental right and are committed to finding solutions that improve access, reduce costs, and enhance the quality of care. Their healthcare proposals include increasing funding for addiction treatment programs, enhancing rural healthcare access, and implementing cost-control measures.

National Security: Ensuring the safety and security of the American people is a top priority for the Trump-Vance partnership. Their national security policies focus on strengthening the military, securing the borders, and addressing emerging threats. They are committed to maintaining a strong and capable defense infrastructure while also pursuing diplomatic solutions to international conflicts.

Social Stability: Promoting social stability and addressing the root causes of social unrest are essential components of the Trump-Vance agenda. They aim to achieve this by addressing issues such as poverty, addiction, and crime through comprehensive and compassionate policies. Their approach emphasizes the importance of community support, education, and economic opportunity in creating a more stable and prosperous society.

The Campaign Strategy

The Trump-Vance campaign strategy is designed to capitalize on their strengths and effectively communicate their vision to the American people. Their approach is multifaceted, combining traditional campaign tactics with innovative outreach methods to build a broad and diverse coalition of supporters.

Grassroots Mobilization: One of the key elements of the Trump-Vance campaign is grassroots mobilization. They recognize the importance of engaging with voters at the local level and building a strong network of supporters. This includes organizing town hall meetings, community events, and door-to-door canvassing efforts. By connecting with voters directly, they aim to build a sense of community and shared purpose.

Media Engagement: Media engagement is another critical component of the campaign strategy. Trump and Vance leverage their media presence to communicate their message and reach a wide audience. This includes appearances on television and radio, as well as active participation on social media platforms. Their goal is to control the narrative and ensure that their vision is clearly articulated to the public.

Policy Proposals: The Trump-Vance campaign places a strong emphasis on policy proposals that address the real concerns of the American people. They have developed a comprehensive platform that outlines their plans for economic growth, healthcare reform, national security, and social stability. By presenting clear and actionable policies, they aim to demonstrate their commitment to making a meaningful impact.

Coalition Building: Building a broad coalition of supporters is essential for the success of the Trump-Vance campaign. They aim to attract voters from across the political spectrum, including independents and disillusioned Democrats. Their focus on addressing the needs of the working class and promoting economic opportunity resonates with a wide range of voters, creating the potential for a diverse and inclusive coalition.

Messaging and Branding: Effective messaging and branding are crucial for the Trump-Vance campaign. They have developed a clear and consistent message that emphasizes their commitment to revitalizing the American Dream and addressing the needs of everyday Americans. Their branding efforts highlight their shared values and the transformative potential of their partnership.

The Impact of the Trump-Vance Partnership

The impact of the Trump-Vance partnership extends beyond the immediate goals of the 2024 election. Their collaboration has the potential to reshape the future of American politics and set a new standard for leadership and governance. By combining experience with innovation, they offer a model for addressing the complex challenges facing the nation.

Revitalizing the American Dream: One of the most significant impacts of the Trump-Vance partnership is their potential to revitalize the American Dream. Their focus on economic growth, job creation, and social stability offers a pathway to renewed prosperity for millions of Americans. By addressing the root causes of poverty and addiction, they aim to create a more equitable and inclusive society.

Restoring Trust in Government: The Trump-Vance partnership also has the potential to restore trust in government. Their commitment to transparency, accountability, and results-oriented governance sets a new standard for political leadership. By delivering on their promises and demonstrating their dedication to the American people, they aim to rebuild confidence in the political system.

Promoting Unity and Inclusivity: The Trump-Vance campaign emphasizes the importance of unity and inclusivity. They recognize that addressing the nation's challenges requires collaboration and cooperation across political and social divides. Their efforts to build a broad and diverse coalition reflect their commitment to promoting a sense of shared purpose and collective responsibility.

Setting a New Direction for the Republican Party: The Trump-Vance partnership represents a new direction for the Republican Party, one that prioritizes the needs of the working class and emphasizes pragmatic solutions to complex problems. Their approach offers a blueprint for the future of the party, one that is grounded in principles of economic opportunity, social stability, and national security.

Conclusion

The alliance between Donald Trump and J.D. Vance represents a bold and innovative approach to addressing the challenges facing America. Their partnership combines the experience and charisma of Trump with the fresh perspective and authenticity of Vance, creating a powerful force for change. Together, they offer a vision for the future that is grounded in the values of the American Dream and a commitment to making a meaningful impact.

As the 2024 election approaches, the Trump-Vance campaign will continue to engage with voters, present their policy proposals, and build a broad coalition of supporters. Their goal is to secure a decisive victory and implement their vision for a revitalized and prosperous America. The journey ahead is filled with challenges, but the potential for transformative change is within reach.

In the following chapters, we will delve deeper into the specific policies and initiatives proposed by the Trump-Vance partnership. We will explore their strategies for economic revitalization, healthcare reform, national security, and social stability, providing a comprehensive understanding of their vision for the future of the United States. Join us as we continue to explore the dynamic and impactful partnership of Donald Trump and J.D. Vance, and discover how their combined efforts could reshape the future of American politics.

Chapter 3: Economic Revitalization - Policies for America's Working Class

Economic revitalization is a cornerstone of the Trump-Vance campaign. The partnership between Donald Trump and J.D. Vance promises to bring about significant changes aimed at rejuvenating American manufacturing, creating sustainable jobs, and ensuring that the benefits of economic growth are shared broadly among all Americans. This chapter delves into the specific economic policies proposed by Trump and Vance, exploring their vision for a revitalized economy and the strategies they plan to implement to achieve it.

The State of the American Economy

To understand the need for economic revitalization, it is essential to examine the current state of the American economy. Over the past few decades, the United States has experienced significant economic shifts, driven by globalization, technological advancements, and changing market dynamics. While these changes have brought about economic growth and innovation, they have also led to challenges such as job displacement, wage stagnation, and increased economic inequality.

The decline of American manufacturing has had a profound impact on communities across the country, particularly in the Rust Belt and Appalachian regions. Factories that once provided stable, well-paying jobs have closed down or moved overseas, leaving behind a legacy of unemployment and economic distress. The rise of automation and the outsourcing of jobs to countries with lower labor costs have further exacerbated these issues.

In addition to the challenges faced by the manufacturing sector, the American economy has also been grappling with the effects of the opioid crisis. The epidemic has devastated communities, contributing to a decline in labor force participation and increased healthcare costs. Addressing these interconnected issues requires a comprehensive approach that tackles the root causes of economic distress and promotes sustainable growth.

The Trump-Vance Economic Vision

The economic vision of Donald Trump and J.D. Vance is centered on the principles of economic nationalism, job creation, and support for the working class. Their policies are designed to stimulate economic growth, enhance competitiveness, and ensure that the benefits of prosperity are broadly shared. Key components of their economic agenda include revitalizing American manufacturing, reducing regulatory burdens, investing in infrastructure, and promoting fair trade practices.

Revitalizing American Manufacturing: One of the primary goals of the Trump-Vance economic agenda is to revitalize American manufacturing. They believe that a strong manufacturing sector is essential for economic stability and national security. To achieve this, they propose a series of measures aimed at supporting domestic production, encouraging innovation, and protecting American industries from unfair competition.

Reducing Regulatory Burdens: Excessive regulations are often cited as a barrier to economic growth and job creation. Trump and Vance advocate for reducing regulatory burdens on businesses, particularly small and medium-sized enterprises. By streamlining regulations and eliminating unnecessary red tape, they aim to create a more business-friendly environment that fosters innovation and entrepreneurship.

Investing in Infrastructure: Infrastructure investment is a key component of the Trump-Vance economic plan. They recognize that modern, efficient infrastructure is critical for economic growth and competitiveness. Their proposals include significant investments in transportation, energy, and digital infrastructure, with a focus on projects that create jobs and stimulate economic activity.

Promoting Fair Trade Practices: Trade policies play a crucial role in shaping the economic landscape. Trump and Vance are committed to promoting fair trade practices that prioritize American interests. They advocate for renegotiating trade deals to ensure that they are fair and beneficial for American workers and businesses. Their approach includes measures to address trade imbalances, protect intellectual property, and combat unfair trade practices by other countries.

Specific Economic Policies and Initiatives

The Trump-Vance economic agenda is comprehensive, encompassing a wide range of policies and initiatives designed to address the challenges facing the American economy. In this section, we will explore some of the specific proposals and strategies that form the core of their economic plan.

1. Tax Reform

Tax reform is a central pillar of the Trump-Vance economic agenda. They believe that a fair and efficient tax system is essential for promoting economic growth and ensuring that the benefits of prosperity are broadly shared. Their tax reform proposals include measures to reduce the tax burden on individuals and businesses, simplify the tax code, and promote investment and job creation.

Key elements of their tax reform plan include:

- **Lowering Corporate Tax Rates:** Reducing the corporate tax rate to make American businesses more competitive on the global stage. By lowering the tax burden on corporations, they aim to encourage investment, innovation, and job creation.

- **Simplifying the Tax Code:** Streamlining the tax code to make it simpler and more transparent. This includes eliminating unnecessary deductions and loopholes, which can create distortions and inefficiencies in the tax system.

- **Incentivizing Investment:** Providing tax incentives for businesses that invest in infrastructure, research and development, and

31

workforce training. These incentives are designed to promote long-term economic growth and competitiveness.

- **Supporting Small Businesses:** Implementing tax measures that specifically support small and medium-sized enterprises, which are the backbone of the American economy. This includes reducing the tax burden on small businesses and providing targeted incentives to help them grow and thrive.

2. Workforce Development

A skilled and capable workforce is essential for economic growth and competitiveness. The Trump-Vance economic agenda includes a strong focus on workforce development, with policies designed to enhance education and training, support vocational and technical education, and ensure that workers have the skills they need to succeed in a rapidly changing economy.

Key elements of their workforce development plan include:

- **Promoting Vocational and Technical Education:** Increasing funding and support for vocational and technical education programs. By providing students with practical skills and training, they aim to prepare them for high-demand jobs in fields such as manufacturing, healthcare, and technology.

- **Expanding Apprenticeships and Training Programs:** Encouraging businesses to invest in apprenticeships and training programs that provide workers with hands-on experience and skills development. This includes offering tax incentives and grants to businesses that participate in these programs.

- **Supporting Lifelong Learning:** Implementing policies that promote lifelong learning and continuous skills development. This includes providing support for workers who want to pursue further education and training throughout their careers.

- **Addressing Workforce Disparities:** Developing targeted initiatives to address workforce disparities and ensure that all Americans have access to opportunities for skills development and career advancement. This includes programs that support underrepresented groups and communities.

3. Innovation and Technology

Innovation and technology are key drivers of economic growth and competitiveness. The Trump-Vance economic agenda includes policies designed to promote innovation, support research and development, and ensure that American businesses remain at the forefront of technological advancements.

Key elements of their innovation and technology plan include:

- **Supporting Research and Development:** Increasing funding for research and development in key areas such as artificial intelligence, biotechnology, and clean energy. By investing in cutting-edge technologies, they aim to drive innovation and create new economic opportunities.

- **Promoting Public-Private Partnerships:** Encouraging collaboration between the public and private sectors to advance technological innovation. This includes supporting initiatives that bring together businesses, government agencies, and academic institutions to develop and commercialize new technologies.

- **Protecting Intellectual Property:** Implementing measures to protect intellectual property rights and ensure that American businesses can compete on a level playing field. This includes strengthening enforcement mechanisms and addressing issues such as patent infringement and trade secret theft.

- **Fostering a Culture of Innovation:** Promoting a culture of innovation and entrepreneurship by supporting initiatives that encourage risk-taking, creativity, and experimentation. This includes providing resources and support for startups and small businesses.

4. Trade and Global Competitiveness

Trade policies play a crucial role in shaping the economic landscape and ensuring that American businesses can compete globally. The Trump-Vance economic agenda includes a strong focus on promoting fair trade practices, addressing trade imbalances, and protecting American industries from unfair competition.

Key elements of their trade and global competitiveness plan include:

- **Renegotiating Trade Deals:** Renegotiating existing trade deals to ensure that they are fair and beneficial for American workers and businesses. This includes addressing issues such as trade imbalances, market access, and labor standards.

- **Combating Unfair Trade Practices:** Implementing measures to combat unfair trade practices by other countries, such as currency manipulation, intellectual property theft, and dumping. This includes strengthening enforcement mechanisms and working with international partners to address these issues.

- **Promoting Export Opportunities:** Supporting initiatives that promote export opportunities for American businesses. This includes providing resources and support for businesses that want to enter international markets and helping them navigate the complexities of global trade.

- **Enhancing Trade Enforcement:** Strengthening trade enforcement mechanisms to ensure that trade agreements are effectively implemented and that American businesses can compete on a level playing field. This includes increasing funding for trade enforcement agencies and improving coordination with international partners.

5. Infrastructure Investment

Investing in infrastructure is a key component of the Trump-Vance economic agenda. They recognize that modern, efficient infrastructure is critical for economic growth and competitiveness. Their infrastructure investment proposals include significant funding for transportation, energy, and digital infrastructure projects.

Key elements of their infrastructure investment plan include:

- **Transportation Infrastructure:** Investing in the modernization and expansion of the transportation infrastructure, including roads, bridges, airports, and public transit systems. This includes funding for projects that enhance connectivity, reduce congestion, and improve safety.

- **Energy Infrastructure:** Supporting initiatives that promote the development and deployment of clean energy technologies. This includes investing in renewable energy sources such as wind, solar, and hydropower, as well as supporting the expansion of the electric grid and energy storage systems.

- **Digital Infrastructure:** Promoting the development of digital infrastructure, including broadband internet access and 5G networks. This includes funding for projects that expand high-speed internet access to underserved and rural areas, as well as initiatives that promote digital literacy and inclusion.

- **Public-Private Partnerships:** Encouraging collaboration between the public and private sectors to finance and develop infrastructure projects. This includes supporting innovative financing mechanisms such as infrastructure bonds and public-private partnerships.

Addressing Economic Inequality

Economic inequality is a significant challenge facing the United States, with disparities in income and wealth contributing to social and economic instability. The Trump-Vance economic agenda includes policies designed to address economic inequality and promote greater economic opportunity for all Americans.

Key elements of their plan to address economic inequality include:

- **Increasing Access to Education and Training:** Promoting policies that increase access to education and training opportunities, particularly for low-income and underrepresented communities. This includes expanding funding for scholarships, grants, and vocational training programs.

- **Supporting Affordable Housing:** Implementing measures to increase the availability of affordable housing and reduce housing costs for low-income families. This includes funding for affordable housing development, rental assistance programs, and initiatives that promote homeownership.

- **Expanding Access to Healthcare:** Promoting policies that increase access to affordable healthcare for all Americans. This includes expanding Medicaid, increasing funding for community health centers, and implementing measures to reduce healthcare costs.

- **Enhancing Social Safety Nets:** Strengthening social safety nets to provide support for individuals and families facing economic hardship. This includes increasing funding for programs such as unemployment insurance, food assistance, and child care support.

The Role of Government and the Private Sector

The Trump-Vance economic agenda emphasizes the importance of collaboration between the government and the private sector in achieving economic revitalization. They believe that a strong partnership between the public and private sectors is essential for addressing the complex challenges facing the American economy and promoting sustainable growth.

Key elements of their approach to public-private collaboration include:

- **Encouraging Investment:** Implementing policies that encourage private sector investment in key areas such as infrastructure, research and development, and workforce training. This includes providing tax incentives, grants, and other forms of support for businesses that invest in these areas.

- **Supporting Innovation and Entrepreneurship:** Promoting a culture of innovation and entrepreneurship by providing resources and support for startups and small businesses. This includes funding for incubators and accelerators, as well as initiatives that promote access to capital and mentorship.

- **Enhancing Regulatory Frameworks:** Implementing regulatory frameworks that promote economic growth and competitiveness while ensuring that businesses operate in a fair and transparent manner. This includes streamlining regulations, reducing compliance costs, and promoting best practices in areas such as environmental protection and worker safety.

- **Fostering Public-Private Partnerships:** Supporting initiatives that promote collaboration between the public and private sectors to address key economic challenges. This includes developing public-private partnerships for infrastructure projects, research and development, and workforce training programs.

Conclusion

The Trump-Vance economic agenda represents a bold and comprehensive approach to addressing the challenges facing the American economy. Their policies are designed to promote economic growth, create jobs, and ensure that the benefits of prosperity are broadly shared among all Americans. By focusing on key areas such as tax reform, workforce development, innovation, trade, and infrastructure investment, they aim to revitalize the American Dream and create a more equitable and prosperous society.

As we continue to explore the specific policies and initiatives proposed by the Trump-Vance partnership, it is clear that their vision for the future of the United States is grounded in the principles of economic nationalism, job creation, and support for the working class. Their commitment to addressing the root causes of economic distress and promoting sustainable growth offers a pathway to renewed prosperity and opportunity for all Americans.

In the next chapter, we will delve into their strategies for combating the opioid epidemic and enhancing healthcare access, providing a comprehensive understanding of their approach to addressing these critical issues. Join us as we continue to explore the dynamic and impactful partnership of Donald Trump and J.D. Vance, and discover how their combined efforts could reshape the future of American politics and society.

Chapter 4: Combating the Opioid Epidemic and Enhancing Healthcare Access

The opioid epidemic is one of the most devastating public health crises facing America today. Its impact has been far-reaching, affecting individuals, families, and entire communities. Addressing this crisis requires a comprehensive and multifaceted approach that goes beyond traditional healthcare solutions. Donald Trump and J.D. Vance have made combating the opioid epidemic and enhancing healthcare access a cornerstone of their campaign. This chapter delves into their strategies and policies for addressing these critical issues, exploring their vision for a healthier America.

The Scope of the Opioid Crisis

The opioid epidemic has claimed the lives of hundreds of thousands of Americans and has left millions more struggling with addiction. The crisis began in the late 1990s, fueled by the over-prescription of opioid painkillers. As the addictive potential of these medications became apparent, regulatory efforts were implemented to curb their availability. However, this led many individuals to turn to illegal opioids such as heroin and synthetic opioids like fentanyl, which are even more potent and dangerous.

The impact of the opioid crisis extends beyond the immediate health consequences. It has strained healthcare systems, increased criminal activity, and burdened social services. The economic cost of the epidemic is staggering, with estimates reaching hundreds of billions of dollars annually. Addressing this crisis requires a coordinated effort that involves healthcare providers, law enforcement, community organizations, and policymakers.

The Trump-Vance Approach to Combating the Opioid Epidemic

Donald Trump and J.D. Vance recognize the urgency of addressing the opioid crisis and have developed a comprehensive approach that includes prevention, treatment, law enforcement, and support for affected individuals and communities. Their strategy aims to reduce the supply of illegal opioids, increase access to treatment and recovery services, and provide support for those impacted by the epidemic.

1. Reducing the Supply of Illegal Opioids

One of the primary goals of the Trump-Vance approach is to reduce the supply of illegal opioids that fuel the epidemic. This involves a combination of law enforcement efforts, regulatory measures, and international cooperation.

- **Strengthening Border Security:** Enhancing border security to prevent the smuggling of illegal opioids into the United States. This includes increasing funding for border patrol agents, investing in advanced detection technologies, and improving coordination with international partners to disrupt drug trafficking networks.

- **Regulating Synthetic Opioids:** Implementing stricter regulations on the production and distribution of synthetic opioids. This includes working with pharmaceutical companies to ensure that these substances are not diverted for illegal use and increasing penalties for those involved in the illegal manufacture and distribution of synthetic opioids.

- **International Cooperation:** Collaborating with international partners to combat the global opioid trade. This includes working with countries such as China and Mexico, which are major sources of synthetic opioids, to improve enforcement efforts and reduce the flow of these substances into the United States.

2. Increasing Access to Treatment and Recovery Services

Effective treatment and recovery services are essential for helping individuals overcome opioid addiction and achieve long-term recovery. The Trump-Vance approach includes measures to increase access to these services and ensure that they are effective and evidence-based.

- **Expanding Treatment Programs:** Increasing funding for treatment programs that provide a range of services, including medication-assisted treatment (MAT), counseling, and behavioral therapies. This includes expanding the availability of MAT, which has been shown to be effective in reducing opioid use and improving recovery outcomes.

- **Improving Access to Recovery Services:** Enhancing access to recovery services that support individuals in their journey to long-term sobriety. This includes funding for recovery housing, peer support programs, and employment and vocational training services that help individuals rebuild their lives after addiction.

- **Supporting Telehealth Services:** Promoting the use of telehealth services to expand access to treatment and recovery services, particularly in rural and underserved areas. This includes increasing funding for telehealth infrastructure and ensuring that healthcare providers are equipped to offer these services.

3. Enhancing Prevention Efforts

Preventing opioid addiction before it starts is a critical component of the Trump-Vance approach. This involves a combination of public education campaigns, prescription monitoring, and community-based initiatives.

- **Public Education Campaigns:** Launching public education campaigns to raise awareness about the risks of opioid use and promote safe medication practices. This includes partnering with schools, community organizations, and media outlets to disseminate information and resources.

- **Prescription Monitoring Programs:** Strengthening prescription monitoring programs to track the prescribing and dispensing of opioids. This includes implementing state-of-the-art monitoring systems that provide real-time data and alerts to healthcare providers about potential cases of misuse or diversion.

- **Community-Based Initiatives:** Supporting community-based initiatives that promote prevention and early intervention. This includes funding for local organizations that provide education, support, and resources to individuals and families affected by opioid addiction.

4. Supporting Individuals and Communities Affected by the Epidemic

The opioid epidemic has had a profound impact on individuals and communities across the United States. The Trump-Vance approach includes measures to provide support and resources to those affected by the crisis.

- **Increasing Funding for Mental Health Services:** Enhancing funding for mental health services to address the co-occurring mental health conditions that often accompany opioid addiction. This includes increasing access to counseling, therapy, and psychiatric services.

- **Supporting Families and Caregivers:** Providing resources and support for families and caregivers of individuals struggling with opioid addiction. This includes funding for support groups, respite care, and educational programs that help families navigate the challenges of addiction.

- **Rebuilding Communities:** Investing in community development initiatives that support recovery and resilience. This includes funding for community centers, job training programs, and housing initiatives that help rebuild communities affected by the opioid crisis.

Enhancing Healthcare Access

In addition to combating the opioid epidemic, the Trump-Vance campaign places a strong emphasis on enhancing healthcare access for all Americans. They recognize that access to quality healthcare is a fundamental right and are committed to implementing policies that improve healthcare access, reduce costs, and enhance the quality of care.

1. Expanding Healthcare Coverage

Expanding healthcare coverage is a key priority for the Trump-Vance campaign. They aim to ensure that all Americans have access to affordable and comprehensive healthcare coverage, regardless of their income or employment status.

- **Expanding Medicaid:** Increasing funding for Medicaid and expanding eligibility to cover more low-income individuals and families. This includes implementing measures to ensure that Medicaid provides comprehensive coverage, including mental health and addiction treatment services.

- **Supporting Private Insurance Options:** Promoting policies that increase access to private insurance options, including employer-sponsored plans and individual market plans. This includes implementing measures to reduce premiums and out-of-pocket costs for individuals and families.

- **Encouraging Health Savings Accounts (HSAs):** Promoting the use of Health Savings Accounts (HSAs) to help individuals save for medical expenses. This includes increasing the contribution limits for HSAs and providing tax incentives for individuals who use these accounts to pay for healthcare expenses.

2. Reducing Healthcare Costs

Reducing healthcare costs is essential for making healthcare more accessible and affordable for all Americans. The Trump-Vance campaign includes measures to address the rising costs of healthcare and ensure that individuals and families can afford the care they need.

- **Implementing Price Transparency:** Promoting price transparency to ensure that patients have access to information about the cost of medical services and procedures. This includes requiring healthcare providers to disclose prices for common services and procedures and implementing measures to ensure that patients receive accurate and understandable information.

- **Negotiating Drug Prices:** Allowing the federal government to negotiate drug prices with pharmaceutical companies to reduce the cost of prescription medications. This includes implementing measures to increase competition and reduce the influence of pharmaceutical companies on drug pricing.

- **Reducing Administrative Costs:** Implementing measures to reduce administrative costs and inefficiencies in the healthcare system. This includes streamlining billing and reimbursement processes, reducing paperwork, and implementing electronic health records systems to improve efficiency and reduce costs.

3. Enhancing Quality of Care

Enhancing the quality of care is essential for improving health outcomes and ensuring that all Americans receive high-quality healthcare. The Trump-Vance campaign includes measures to promote evidence-based practices, improve healthcare delivery, and ensure that healthcare providers are equipped to deliver high-quality care.

- **Promoting Evidence-Based Practices:** Implementing measures to promote evidence-based practices and ensure that healthcare providers use the most effective and up-to-date treatments and interventions. This includes increasing funding for research and clinical trials and providing resources and support for healthcare providers to implement evidence-based practices.

- **Improving Healthcare Delivery:** Implementing measures to improve healthcare delivery and ensure that patients receive timely and coordinated care. This includes promoting integrated care models that bring together primary care, specialty care, and mental health services and supporting initiatives that improve care coordination and communication among healthcare providers.

- **Supporting Healthcare Providers:** Providing resources and support for healthcare providers to ensure that they are equipped to deliver high-quality care. This includes increasing funding for medical education and training programs, providing financial incentives for healthcare providers who deliver high-quality care, and implementing measures to address burnout and improve working conditions for healthcare providers.

4. Addressing Health Disparities

Addressing health disparities is essential for ensuring that all Americans have access to quality healthcare, regardless of their race, ethnicity, or socioeconomic status. The Trump-Vance campaign includes measures to address health disparities and promote health equity.

- **Increasing Access to Care in Underserved Areas:** Implementing measures to increase access to healthcare in underserved areas, including rural and low-income communities. This includes increasing funding for community health centers, expanding telehealth services, and providing incentives for healthcare providers to practice in underserved areas.

- **Promoting Cultural Competency:** Promoting cultural competency among healthcare providers to ensure that they are equipped to deliver care that is respectful and responsive to the cultural and linguistic needs of their patients. This includes increasing funding for cultural competency training programs and implementing measures to promote diversity in the healthcare workforce.

- **Addressing Social Determinants of Health:** Implementing measures to address the social determinants of health, such as housing, education, and employment. This includes funding for programs that provide social services and support to individuals and families and implementing policies that promote economic and social stability.

The Role of Technology in Healthcare

Technology plays a crucial role in enhancing healthcare access and improving health outcomes. The Trump-Vance campaign includes measures to promote the use of technology in healthcare and ensure that healthcare providers have access to the tools and resources they need to deliver high-quality care.

1. Promoting Telehealth Services

Telehealth services have the potential to expand access to healthcare, particularly in rural and underserved areas. The Trump-Vance campaign includes measures to promote the use of telehealth services and ensure that healthcare providers are equipped to offer these services.

- **Increasing Funding for Telehealth Infrastructure:** Increasing funding for telehealth infrastructure, including broadband internet access and telehealth equipment. This includes providing grants and loans to healthcare providers to support the implementation of telehealth services.

- **Expanding Reimbursement for Telehealth Services:** Expanding reimbursement for telehealth services to ensure that healthcare providers are fairly compensated for delivering care via telehealth. This includes implementing measures to ensure that telehealth services are reimbursed at the same rate as in-person services.

- **Promoting Telehealth Education and Training:** Providing resources and support for healthcare providers to ensure that they are equipped to deliver care via telehealth. This includes increasing funding for telehealth education and training programs and implementing measures to promote best practices in telehealth delivery.

2. Implementing Electronic Health Records (EHRs)

Electronic Health Records (EHRs) have the potential to improve healthcare delivery and enhance the quality of care. The Trump-Vance campaign includes measures to promote the implementation of EHRs and ensure that healthcare providers have access to the tools and resources they need to use EHRs effectively.

- **Increasing Funding for EHR Implementation:** Increasing funding for EHR implementation, including grants and loans to healthcare providers to support the adoption of EHR systems. This includes providing financial incentives for healthcare providers who implement EHRs and achieve meaningful use standards.

- **Promoting Interoperability:** Promoting interoperability to ensure that EHR systems can communicate and share information across different healthcare providers and settings. This includes implementing standards for data exchange and promoting the use of health information exchanges (HIEs) to facilitate the sharing of patient information.

- **Ensuring Data Security and Privacy:** Implementing measures to ensure the security and privacy of patient information in EHR systems. This includes implementing robust data security protocols, providing resources and support for healthcare providers to protect patient information, and ensuring that patients have control over their own health information.

The Future of Healthcare in America

The Trump-Vance approach to combating the opioid epidemic and enhancing healthcare access represents a bold and comprehensive vision for the future of healthcare in America. Their policies are designed to address the immediate needs of individuals and communities affected by the opioid crisis, while also promoting long-term health and wellness for all Americans.

By focusing on prevention, treatment, and recovery, they aim to reduce the impact of the opioid epidemic and support individuals in their journey to long-term sobriety. Their approach to healthcare access emphasizes the importance of expanding coverage, reducing costs, and enhancing the quality of care, ensuring that all Americans have access to the healthcare services they need.

As the Trump-Vance campaign continues to engage with voters and present their policy proposals, it is clear that their vision for the future of healthcare in America is grounded in the principles of compassion, innovation, and equity. Their commitment to addressing the root causes of health disparities and promoting health equity offers a pathway to a healthier and more prosperous society.

In the next chapter, we will explore their strategies for national security and defense, providing a comprehensive understanding of their approach to ensuring the safety and security of the American people. Join us as we continue to explore the dynamic and impactful partnership of Donald Trump and J.D. Vance, and discover how their combined efforts could reshape the future of American politics and society.

Chapter 5: National Security and Defense

Ensuring the safety and security of the American people is a top priority for the Trump-Vance campaign. Their approach to national security and defense is comprehensive, focusing on strengthening the military, securing the borders, addressing emerging threats, and promoting diplomatic solutions to international conflicts. This chapter delves into their strategies and policies for safeguarding the nation and explores how they plan to navigate the complex global security landscape.

The Importance of a Strong National Defense

A strong national defense is essential for protecting the sovereignty and interests of the United States. The Trump-Vance campaign recognizes that a capable and well-equipped military is the cornerstone of national security. Their defense policies are designed to ensure that the U.S. Armed Forces remain the most powerful and effective military in the world, capable of responding to a wide range of threats and challenges.

Key elements of their national defense strategy include increasing defense spending, modernizing the military, enhancing readiness and capabilities, and supporting the welfare of military personnel and their families.

Increasing Defense Spending

One of the primary goals of the Trump-Vance defense strategy is to increase defense spending to ensure that the U.S. military has the resources it needs to maintain its superiority. This includes funding for new equipment, advanced technologies, personnel training, and infrastructure improvements.

- **Modernizing Equipment and Technology:** Investing in the modernization of military equipment and technology is crucial for

49

maintaining a competitive edge. This includes funding for the development and procurement of advanced weaponry, such as next-generation fighter jets, naval vessels, and missile defense systems. Additionally, it involves investing in emerging technologies, such as artificial intelligence, cybersecurity, and space capabilities, to address evolving threats.

- **Enhancing Readiness and Training:** Ensuring that military personnel are well-trained and ready to respond to threats is a key component of the Trump-Vance defense strategy. This includes increasing funding for training programs, joint exercises, and simulations that prepare troops for a wide range of scenarios. Additionally, it involves improving the infrastructure and facilities used for training and operations.

- **Supporting Military Research and Development:** Investing in research and development (R&D) is essential for maintaining technological superiority. The Trump-Vance campaign plans to increase funding for R&D initiatives that focus on developing cutting-edge technologies and capabilities. This includes partnerships with private industry, academic institutions, and international allies to foster innovation and accelerate the development of new technologies.

Strengthening Military Capabilities

Strengthening the capabilities of the U.S. military is a central aspect of the Trump-Vance defense strategy. This involves enhancing the capabilities of all branches of the military, ensuring that they are equipped to handle a wide range of threats and challenges.

- **Army and Ground Forces:** Enhancing the capabilities of the Army and ground forces is essential for responding to conventional and unconventional threats. This includes increasing the size of the Army, modernizing equipment, and improving mobility and logistics. Additionally, it involves investing in special operations forces to enhance their ability to conduct counterterrorism and unconventional warfare missions.

- **Navy and Maritime Forces:** Strengthening the capabilities of the Navy and maritime forces is crucial for maintaining maritime security and projecting power globally. This includes expanding the size of the fleet, modernizing naval vessels, and investing in advanced maritime technologies. Additionally, it involves enhancing the capabilities of the Marine Corps to conduct amphibious operations and support joint force missions.

- **Air Force and Aerospace Forces:** Ensuring the superiority of the Air Force and aerospace forces is vital for maintaining air dominance and addressing emerging threats. This includes funding for new aircraft, unmanned aerial systems, and space capabilities. Additionally, it involves investing in advanced missile defense systems to protect against ballistic and hypersonic missile threats.

- **Cybersecurity and Information Warfare:** Addressing cybersecurity and information warfare threats is a critical component of the Trump-Vance defense strategy. This includes increasing funding for cybersecurity initiatives, enhancing the capabilities of cyber forces, and improving the resilience of critical infrastructure. Additionally, it involves developing strategies to counter disinformation and influence operations conducted by adversaries.

Supporting Military Personnel and Families

Supporting the welfare of military personnel and their families is a key priority for the Trump-Vance campaign. They recognize that a strong and capable military is built on the dedication and commitment of its service members and their families. Their policies aim to ensure that military personnel receive the support and resources they need to succeed.

- **Improving Compensation and Benefits:** Ensuring that military personnel are fairly compensated for their service is essential for maintaining morale and retention. The Trump-Vance campaign plans to increase pay and benefits for service members, including housing allowances, healthcare, and retirement benefits. Additionally, it involves providing support for veterans through programs that assist with employment, education, and healthcare.

- **Enhancing Family Support Programs:** Providing support for military families is crucial for ensuring the well-being of service members. This includes funding for family support programs, such as childcare, education, and mental health services. Additionally, it involves implementing initiatives that support the spouses and children of service members, helping them navigate the challenges of military life.

- **Addressing Mental Health and Wellness:** Ensuring the mental health and wellness of military personnel is a key priority. The Trump-Vance campaign plans to increase funding for mental health services, including counseling, therapy, and support programs. Additionally, it involves implementing measures to reduce the stigma associated with seeking mental health care and promoting a culture of wellness within the military.

Securing the Borders

Securing the borders is a critical aspect of the Trump-Vance national security strategy. They recognize that a secure border is essential for protecting the sovereignty of the United States and preventing the entry of illegal immigrants, drugs, and other threats. Their approach to border security includes a combination of physical barriers, technological solutions, and enhanced enforcement measures.

- **Building Physical Barriers:** Constructing physical barriers, such as walls and fences, is a key component of the Trump-Vance border security strategy. They believe that physical barriers are an effective way to prevent illegal crossings and enhance the overall security of the border. This includes continuing the construction of the border wall along the U.S.-Mexico border and improving existing barriers.

- **Implementing Technological Solutions:** Utilizing advanced technologies to enhance border security is another critical element of their strategy. This includes deploying surveillance systems, drones, and sensors to monitor the border and detect illegal activity. Additionally, it involves investing in biometric technologies to improve the identification and tracking of individuals entering and exiting the country.

- **Enhancing Border Enforcement:** Increasing funding and resources for border enforcement agencies, such as U.S. Customs and Border Protection (CBP) and Immigration and Customs Enforcement (ICE), is essential for ensuring effective border security. This includes hiring additional agents, providing advanced training, and improving the capabilities of enforcement agencies to respond to threats.

- **Promoting Legal Immigration:** While securing the borders, the Trump-Vance campaign also emphasizes the importance of promoting legal immigration. They believe that a well-regulated immigration system is essential for ensuring that individuals who contribute to the economy and society can enter the country legally. This includes implementing measures to streamline the immigration process, reduce backlogs, and promote skilled immigration.

Addressing Emerging Threats

Addressing emerging threats is a critical component of the Trump-Vance national security strategy. They recognize that the global security landscape is constantly evolving, with new threats emerging from state and non-state actors. Their approach includes developing strategies to address these threats and ensure that the United States remains prepared to respond to a wide range of challenges.

- **Countering Terrorism:** Combating terrorism remains a top priority for the Trump-Vance campaign. This includes enhancing the capabilities of counterterrorism forces, improving intelligence gathering and sharing, and disrupting terrorist financing networks.

Additionally, it involves working with international partners to address the root causes of terrorism and promote stability in regions affected by terrorist activity.

- **Deterring Aggression from Adversaries:** Deterring aggression from state actors, such as China, Russia, and Iran, is essential for maintaining global stability. The Trump-Vance campaign plans to enhance the capabilities of the U.S. military to deter and respond to aggression, including increasing the presence of U.S. forces in key regions and conducting joint exercises with allies. Additionally, it involves developing strategies to counter the influence and coercive activities of adversaries.

- **Addressing Cybersecurity Threats:** Cybersecurity is a critical component of the Trump-Vance national security strategy. This includes increasing funding for cybersecurity initiatives, enhancing the capabilities of cyber forces, and improving the resilience of critical infrastructure. Additionally, it involves developing strategies to counter cyberattacks and influence operations conducted by state and non-state actors.

- **Promoting Space Security:** Ensuring the security of space assets is essential for maintaining national security and economic stability. The Trump-Vance campaign plans to increase funding for space capabilities, including satellite defense systems and space situational awareness. Additionally, it involves developing strategies to protect space assets from adversarial activities and promoting international norms for the responsible use of space.

Promoting Diplomatic Solutions

While maintaining a strong national defense, the Trump-Vance campaign also emphasizes the importance of promoting diplomatic solutions to international conflicts. They believe that diplomacy is an essential tool for preventing and resolving conflicts, promoting stability, and advancing U.S. interests.

- **Strengthening Alliances and Partnerships:** Strengthening alliances and partnerships with key allies is a critical component of the Trump-Vance diplomatic strategy. This includes enhancing cooperation with NATO allies, fostering partnerships in the Indo-Pacific region, and promoting regional security initiatives. Additionally, it involves working with international organizations, such as the United Nations, to address global challenges.

- **Engaging in Multilateral Diplomacy:** Engaging in multilateral diplomacy is essential for addressing complex global issues, such as climate change, nuclear proliferation, and global health. The Trump-Vance campaign plans to actively participate in multilateral forums and work with international partners to develop coordinated responses to these challenges.

- **Promoting Trade and Economic Diplomacy:** Promoting trade and economic diplomacy is essential for advancing U.S. economic interests and enhancing global stability. This includes negotiating trade agreements that promote fair and reciprocal trade, addressing trade imbalances, and supporting economic development in key regions. Additionally, it involves using economic tools, such as sanctions and incentives, to influence the behavior of adversaries.

- **Supporting Conflict Resolution and Peacebuilding:** Supporting conflict resolution and peacebuilding efforts is essential for promoting stability and preventing the resurgence of violence. The Trump-Vance campaign plans to increase funding for peacekeeping and stabilization operations, support mediation and negotiation efforts, and provide assistance for post-conflict reconstruction and development.

Conclusion

The Trump-Vance approach to national security and defense represents a comprehensive and multifaceted strategy for safeguarding the United States. Their policies are designed to ensure that the U.S. military remains the most powerful and effective force in the world, capable of responding to a wide range of threats and challenges. By focusing on strengthening military capabilities, securing the borders, addressing emerging threats, and promoting diplomatic solutions, they aim to create a safer and more secure nation.

As the Trump-Vance campaign continues to engage with voters and present their policy proposals, it is clear that their vision for the future of national security is grounded in the principles of strength, preparedness, and collaboration. Their commitment to maintaining a strong national defense, supporting military personnel and their families, and promoting global stability offers a pathway to a more secure and prosperous future for all Americans.

In the next chapter, we will explore their strategies for social justice and equality, providing a comprehensive understanding of their approach to addressing these critical issues. Join us as we continue to explore the dynamic and impactful partnership of Donald Trump and J.D. Vance, and discover how their combined efforts could reshape the future of American politics and society.

Chapter 6: Social Justice and Equality

Social justice and equality are at the heart of many of the challenges facing the United States today. These issues encompass a wide range of topics, from racial and gender equality to economic and educational opportunities. The Trump-Vance campaign recognizes the importance of addressing these challenges and has developed a comprehensive approach to promoting social justice and equality. This chapter delves into their strategies and policies, exploring their vision for a more just and equitable America.

The State of Social Justice in America

Social justice in America has been a contentious issue for many years, with deep-rooted systemic inequalities affecting various aspects of society. Despite significant progress over the decades, disparities in income, education, healthcare, and criminal justice persist, disproportionately impacting marginalized communities.

Economic inequality remains a pressing concern, with wealth and income gaps widening between the rich and the poor. Access to quality education and healthcare continues to be uneven, often influenced by factors such as race, geography, and socioeconomic status. The criminal justice system has faced criticism for its treatment of minorities and low-income individuals, with issues such as mass incarceration and police brutality sparking nationwide protests.

Addressing these complex and interrelated issues requires a multifaceted approach that encompasses policy changes, community engagement, and a commitment to fairness and justice. The Trump-Vance campaign aims to tackle these challenges head-on, with policies designed to promote equality and opportunity for all Americans.

Economic Equality and Opportunity

Promoting economic equality and opportunity is a cornerstone of the Trump-Vance approach to social justice. They believe that ensuring all Americans have access to economic opportunities is essential for creating a more just and equitable society. Their policies focus on addressing income inequality, supporting small businesses, and promoting job creation and workforce development.

1. Addressing Income Inequality

Income inequality is a significant barrier to social justice, with disparities in income contributing to broader social and economic inequalities. The Trump-Vance campaign has developed policies aimed at reducing income inequality and ensuring that all Americans have the opportunity to achieve economic success.

- **Raising the Minimum Wage:** Implementing a gradual increase in the federal minimum wage to ensure that all workers receive fair compensation for their labor. This includes providing support for small businesses to help them adapt to the increased labor costs and ensuring that the minimum wage keeps pace with inflation.

- **Tax Reform for the Working Class:** Implementing tax reforms that benefit low- and middle-income individuals and families. This includes expanding tax credits, such as the Earned Income Tax Credit (EITC) and the Child Tax Credit, to provide financial support to working families and reduce their tax burden.

- **Supporting Wage Growth:** Promoting policies that support wage growth and reduce income inequality. This includes encouraging businesses to adopt fair wage practices, supporting collective bargaining rights, and implementing measures to close the gender and racial pay gaps.

2. Supporting Small Businesses

Small businesses are the backbone of the American economy, providing jobs and economic opportunities in communities across the country. The Trump-Vance campaign recognizes the importance of supporting small businesses and has developed policies aimed at helping them thrive.

- **Access to Capital:** Increasing access to capital for small businesses through expanded loan programs, grants, and tax incentives. This includes supporting initiatives that provide funding for startups and entrepreneurs, particularly those from underrepresented communities.

- **Reducing Regulatory Burdens:** Implementing measures to reduce the regulatory burdens on small businesses, making it easier for them to operate and grow. This includes streamlining regulations, reducing compliance costs, and providing resources and support to help small businesses navigate regulatory requirements.

- **Promoting Entrepreneurship:** Encouraging entrepreneurship through initiatives that provide training, mentorship, and support for aspiring business owners. This includes funding for entrepreneurship education programs and supporting incubators and accelerators that help startups succeed.

3. Job Creation and Workforce Development

Creating jobs and supporting workforce development is essential for promoting economic equality and opportunity. The Trump-Vance campaign has developed policies aimed at creating jobs, supporting workforce training, and ensuring that all Americans have the skills they need to succeed in the modern economy.

- **Infrastructure Investment:** Investing in infrastructure projects that create jobs and stimulate economic growth. This includes funding for transportation, energy, and digital infrastructure projects that provide employment opportunities and improve the overall competitiveness of the economy.

- **Vocational and Technical Education:** Increasing funding and support for vocational and technical education programs that provide students with practical skills and training. This includes expanding apprenticeship programs and providing incentives for businesses to invest in workforce training.

- **Workforce Development Programs:** Implementing workforce development programs that provide training and support for individuals seeking to enter or reenter the workforce. This includes funding for job training programs, career counseling, and job placement services.

Education and Access to Opportunity

Access to quality education is a fundamental aspect of social justice and equality. The Trump-Vance campaign recognizes the importance of providing all Americans with access to educational opportunities and has developed policies aimed at improving the education system, supporting students, and ensuring that everyone has the chance to succeed.

1. Improving K-12 Education

Improving the quality of K-12 education is essential for ensuring that all students have the opportunity to succeed. The Trump-Vance campaign has developed policies aimed at addressing disparities in education, supporting teachers, and promoting student achievement.

- **Addressing Disparities in Education:** Implementing measures to address disparities in education and ensure that all students have access to quality education. This includes increasing funding for schools in low-income areas, reducing class sizes, and providing resources and support for disadvantaged students.

- **Supporting Teachers:** Providing support for teachers to ensure that they have the resources and training they need to succeed. This includes increasing funding for teacher salaries, providing professional development opportunities, and implementing measures to reduce teacher burnout and turnover.

- **Promoting Student Achievement:** Implementing initiatives that promote student achievement and ensure that all students have the opportunity to succeed. This includes expanding access to early childhood education, providing support for students with disabilities, and implementing measures to improve academic outcomes.

2. Expanding Access to Higher Education

Access to higher education is a key factor in promoting economic opportunity and social mobility.. The Trump-Vance campaign has developed policies aimed at expanding access to higher education and ensuring that all students have the opportunity to pursue their educational goals.

- **Increasing Financial Aid:** Expanding financial aid programs to make higher education more affordable for low- and middle-income students. This includes increasing funding for Pell Grants, providing support for work-study programs, and implementing measures to reduce student loan debt.

- **Supporting Community Colleges:** Providing support for community colleges to ensure that they can offer high-quality education and training programs. This includes increasing funding for community colleges, expanding access to dual enrollment programs, and providing support for students who transfer to four-year institutions.

- **Promoting Workforce Development:** Implementing initiatives that promote workforce development and ensure that students are prepared for the demands of the modern economy. This includes funding for vocational and technical education programs, supporting apprenticeships and internships, and providing resources and support for career and technical education.

Healthcare Access and Equity

Access to quality healthcare is a fundamental aspect of social justice and equality. The Trump-Vance campaign recognizes the importance of ensuring that all Americans have access to affordable and comprehensive healthcare and has developed policies aimed at addressing disparities in healthcare access and promoting health equity.

1. Expanding Healthcare Coverage

Expanding healthcare coverage is essential for ensuring that all Americans have access to the care they need. The Trump-Vance campaign has developed policies aimed at increasing healthcare coverage and ensuring that no one is left without access to essential healthcare services.

- **Expanding Medicaid:** Increasing funding for Medicaid and expanding eligibility to cover more low-income individuals and families. This includes implementing measures to ensure that Medicaid provides comprehensive coverage, including mental health and addiction treatment services.

- **Supporting Private Insurance Options:** Promoting policies that increase access to private insurance options, including employer-sponsored plans and individual market plans. This includes implementing measures to reduce premiums and out-of-pocket costs for individuals and families.

- **Encouraging Health Savings Accounts (HSAs):** Promoting the use of Health Savings Accounts (HSAs) to help individuals save for medical expenses. This includes increasing the contribution limits for HSAs and providing tax incentives for individuals who use these accounts to pay for healthcare expenses.

2. Reducing Healthcare Costs

Reducing healthcare costs is essential for making healthcare more accessible and affordable for all Americans. The Trump-Vance campaign includes measures to address the rising costs of healthcare and ensure that individuals and families can afford the care they need.

- **Implementing Price Transparency:** Promoting price transparency to ensure that patients have access to information about the cost of medical services and procedures. This includes requiring healthcare providers to disclose prices for common services and procedures and implementing measures to ensure that patients receive accurate and understandable information.

- **Negotiating Drug Prices:** Allowing the federal government to negotiate drug prices with pharmaceutical companies to reduce the cost of prescription medications. This includes implementing measures to increase competition and reduce the influence of pharmaceutical companies on drug pricing.

- **Reducing Administrative Costs:** Implementing measures to reduce administrative costs and inefficiencies in the healthcare system. This includes streamlining billing and reimbursement processes, reducing paperwork, and implementing electronic health records systems to improve efficiency and reduce costs.

3. Enhancing Quality of Care

Enhancing the quality of care is essential for improving health outcomes and ensuring that all Americans receive high-quality healthcare. The Trump-Vance campaign includes measures to promote evidence-based practices, improve healthcare delivery, and ensure that healthcare providers are equipped to deliver high-quality care.

- **Promoting Evidence-Based Practices:** Implementing measures to promote evidence-based practices and ensure that healthcare providers use the most effective and up-to-date treatments and interventions. This includes increasing funding for research and clinical trials and providing resources and support for healthcare providers to implement evidence-based practices.

- **Improving Healthcare Delivery:** Implementing measures to improve healthcare delivery and ensure that patients receive timely and coordinated care. This includes promoting integrated care models that bring together primary care, specialty care, and mental health services and supporting initiatives that improve care coordination and communication among healthcare providers.

- **Supporting Healthcare Providers:** Providing resources and support for healthcare providers to ensure that they are equipped to deliver high-quality care. This includes increasing funding for medical education and training programs, providing financial incentives for healthcare providers who deliver high-quality care, and implementing measures to address burnout and improve working conditions for healthcare providers.

4. Addressing Health Disparities

Addressing health disparities is essential for ensuring that all Americans have access to quality healthcare, regardless of their race, ethnicity, or socioeconomic status. The Trump-Vance campaign includes measures to address health disparities and promote health equity.

- **Increasing Access to Care in Underserved Areas:** Implementing measures to increase access to healthcare in underserved areas, including rural and low-income communities. This includes increasing funding for community health centers, expanding telehealth services, and providing incentives for healthcare providers to practice in underserved areas.

- **Promoting Cultural Competency:** Promoting cultural competency among healthcare providers to ensure that they are equipped to deliver care that is respectful and responsive to the cultural and linguistic needs of their patients. This includes increasing funding for cultural competency training programs and implementing measures to promote diversity in the healthcare workforce.

- **Addressing Social Determinants of Health:** Implementing measures to address the social determinants of health, such as housing, education, and employment. This includes funding for programs that provide social services and support to individuals and families and implementing policies that promote economic and social stability.

Criminal Justice Reform

Criminal justice reform is a critical aspect of promoting social justice and equality. The Trump-Vance campaign recognizes the importance of addressing disparities in the criminal justice system and has developed policies aimed at promoting fairness, reducing mass incarceration, and ensuring that the justice system works for all Americans.

1. Reducing Mass Incarceration

Reducing mass incarceration is essential for promoting social justice and addressing the disparities in the criminal justice system. The Trump-Vance campaign includes measures to reduce the prison population and ensure that individuals receive fair and just treatment.

- **Sentencing Reform:** Implementing sentencing reform to reduce mandatory minimum sentences and promote alternatives to incarceration. This includes providing judges with greater discretion in sentencing and implementing measures to ensure that sentences are proportionate to the offenses committed.

- **Expanding Alternatives to Incarceration:** Promoting alternatives to incarceration, such as drug courts, mental health courts, and diversion programs. This includes increasing funding for these programs and providing support for individuals who participate in them.

- **Improving Reentry Programs:** Supporting reentry programs that help individuals transition back into society after incarceration. This includes funding for job training, education, and housing programs that support successful reentry and reduce recidivism.

2. Promoting Fairness in the Criminal Justice System

Ensuring fairness in the criminal justice system is essential for promoting social justice and equality. The Trump-Vance campaign includes measures to address disparities in the justice system and ensure that all individuals receive fair and just treatment.

- **Addressing Racial Disparities:** Implementing measures to address racial disparities in the criminal justice system and ensure that individuals are not treated unfairly based on their race or ethnicity. This includes increasing funding for bias training programs and implementing measures to promote diversity in the justice system.

- **Promoting Police Accountability:** Enhancing police accountability to ensure that law enforcement officers are held accountable for their actions. This includes implementing measures to increase transparency, such as body cameras and independent oversight, and promoting community policing initiatives that build trust between law enforcement and the communities they serve.

- **Ensuring Access to Legal Representation:** Ensuring that all individuals have access to quality legal representation, regardless of their ability to pay. This includes increasing funding for public defender programs and implementing measures to reduce the burden of court fees and fines on low-income individuals.

3. Supporting Victims of Crime

Supporting victims of crime is a critical aspect of promoting social justice and ensuring that the justice system works for all individuals. The Trump-Vance campaign includes measures to provide support and resources for victims of crime and ensure that their needs are addressed.

- **Increasing Funding for Victim Services:** Increasing funding for victim services programs that provide support and resources for victims of crime. This includes funding for counseling, legal assistance, and housing support for victims of domestic violence, sexual assault, and other crimes.

- **Promoting Restorative Justice:** Implementing restorative justice programs that promote healing and reconciliation for victims and offenders. This includes funding for programs that facilitate dialogue and mediation between victims and offenders and provide opportunities for restitution and rehabilitation.

- **Ensuring Victim Rights:** Ensuring that victims of crime have their rights protected and are treated with dignity and respect. This includes implementing measures to ensure that victims are informed of their rights and have access to the resources and support they need.

Promoting Gender Equality

Promoting gender equality is essential for creating a more just and equitable society. The Trump-Vance campaign recognizes the importance of addressing gender disparities and has developed policies aimed at promoting equality and opportunity for all individuals, regardless of their gender.

1. Addressing the Gender Pay Gap

Addressing the gender pay gap is essential for promoting economic equality and ensuring that all individuals receive fair compensation for their work. The Trump-Vance campaign includes measures to promote pay equity and reduce the gender pay gap.

- **Promoting Pay Transparency:** Implementing measures to promote pay transparency and ensure that individuals have access to information about pay practices. This includes requiring employers to disclose pay data and implementing measures to address pay disparities.

- **Supporting Pay Equity Legislation:** Supporting legislation that promotes pay equity and addresses the gender pay gap. This includes implementing measures to ensure that women receive equal pay for equal work and providing support for initiatives that promote pay equity.

- **Encouraging Employer Practices:** Encouraging employers to adopt practices that promote pay equity and reduce the gender pay gap. This includes providing resources and support for employers to implement pay equity initiatives and promoting best practices in pay equity.

2. Supporting Women in the Workforce

Supporting women in the workforce is essential for promoting gender equality and ensuring that all individuals have the opportunity to succeed. The Trump-Vance campaign includes measures to support women in the workforce and promote gender equality.

- **Promoting Family-Friendly Policies:** Implementing policies that support work-life balance and promote gender equality in the workplace. This includes expanding access to paid family leave, promoting flexible work arrangements, and providing support for child care and elder care.

- **Supporting Women in Leadership:** Promoting initiatives that support women in leadership and ensure that women have access to opportunities for career advancement. This includes funding for leadership development programs, mentoring initiatives, and networking opportunities for women.

- **Addressing Workplace Discrimination:** Implementing measures to address workplace discrimination and ensure that individuals are not treated unfairly based on their gender. This includes increasing funding for enforcement of anti-discrimination laws and promoting diversity and inclusion initiatives in the workplace.

3. Promoting Health and Well-Being for Women

Promoting the health and well-being of women is essential for ensuring that all individuals have the opportunity to lead healthy and fulfilling lives. The Trump-Vance campaign includes measures to address the health and well-being of women and promote gender equality in healthcare.

- **Increasing Access to Women's Health Services:** Increasing access to comprehensive women's health services, including reproductive health, prenatal care, and preventive care. This includes funding for women's health clinics, expanding access to contraception, and promoting initiatives that support maternal and child health.

- **Supporting Mental Health for Women:** Providing support for mental health services that address the unique needs of women. This includes funding for counseling and therapy services, promoting initiatives that address mental health stigma, and providing support for women who experience mental health challenges.

- **Addressing Gender-Based Violence:** Implementing measures to address gender-based violence and ensure that women are protected from violence and abuse. This includes increasing funding for domestic violence shelters, providing support for victims of sexual assault, and implementing measures to prevent and address gender-based violence.

Conclusion

The Trump-Vance approach to social justice and equality represents a comprehensive and multifaceted strategy for promoting fairness and opportunity for all Americans. Their policies are designed to address the root causes of inequality, support marginalized communities, and ensure that all individuals have the opportunity to succeed.

By focusing on economic equality, education, healthcare access, criminal justice reform, and gender equality, the Trump-Vance campaign aims to create a more just and equitable society. Their commitment to addressing disparities and promoting social justice offers a pathway to a brighter and more inclusive future for all Americans.

As we continue to explore the specific policies and initiatives proposed by the Trump-Vance partnership, it is clear that their vision for the future of the United States is grounded in the principles of fairness, opportunity, and justice. Their commitment to promoting social justice and equality offers a pathway to a more just and equitable society for all.

In the next chapter, we will explore their strategies for tax reform and economic policy, providing a comprehensive understanding of their approach to promoting economic growth and prosperity. Join us as we continue to explore the dynamic and impactful partnership of Donald Trump and J.D. Vance, and discover how their combined efforts could reshape the future of American politics and society.

Chapter 7: Tax Reform and Economic Policy

Economic policy and tax reform are central components of the Trump-Vance campaign. Their approach focuses on stimulating economic growth, creating jobs, and ensuring that the benefits of prosperity are broadly shared across all segments of society. This chapter delves into their comprehensive economic strategy, exploring their vision for a more vibrant and equitable economy and the specific policies they propose to achieve these goals.

The Current State of the U.S. Economy

The U.S. economy has undergone significant changes over the past few decades. While technological advancements and globalization have driven growth and innovation, they have also contributed to economic disparities and job displacement. The COVID-19 pandemic further exacerbated these issues, leading to widespread unemployment and economic uncertainty.

As the economy recovers from the pandemic, there is a pressing need to address the underlying structural issues that contribute to economic inequality and stagnation. The Trump-Vance campaign aims to tackle these challenges head-on with a bold and comprehensive economic agenda.

The Trump-Vance Economic Vision

The economic vision of Donald Trump and J.D. Vance is centered on the principles of economic nationalism, job creation, and support for the working class. Their policies are designed to stimulate economic growth, enhance competitiveness, and ensure that the benefits of prosperity are shared broadly. Key components of their economic agenda include tax reform, regulatory relief, infrastructure investment, and support for small businesses.

Tax Reform

Tax reform is a cornerstone of the Trump-Vance economic agenda. They believe that a fair and efficient tax system is essential for promoting economic growth and ensuring that the benefits of prosperity are broadly shared. Their tax reform proposals include measures to reduce the tax burden on individuals and businesses, simplify the tax code, and promote investment and job creation.

1. Reducing Corporate Tax Rates

One of the primary goals of the Trump-Vance tax reform plan is to reduce the corporate tax rate to make American businesses more competitive on the global stage. By lowering the tax burden on corporations, they aim to encourage investment, innovation, and job creation.

- **Encouraging Domestic Investment:** Lowering the corporate tax rate to encourage businesses to invest in domestic operations. This includes expanding production facilities, investing in research and development, and hiring additional workers.

- **Attracting Foreign Investment:** Making the U.S. a more attractive destination for foreign investment by offering a competitive corporate tax rate. This includes providing incentives for multinational companies to establish or expand their operations in the U.S.

2. Simplifying the Tax Code

Simplifying the tax code is essential for making it easier for individuals and businesses to comply with tax laws and reducing the administrative burden on taxpayers. The Trump-Vance tax reform plan includes measures to streamline the tax code and eliminate unnecessary deductions and loopholes.

- **Reducing Complexity:** Simplifying the tax code by reducing the number of tax brackets and eliminating redundant provisions. This includes consolidating tax credits and deductions to create a more straightforward and transparent tax system.

- **Eliminating Loopholes:** Closing tax loopholes that allow individuals and businesses to avoid paying their fair share of taxes. This includes implementing measures to prevent tax evasion and ensure that all taxpayers contribute to the funding of essential public services.

3. Promoting Investment and Job Creation

Promoting investment and job creation is a key priority of the Trump-Vance tax reform plan. They believe that providing tax incentives for businesses to invest in infrastructure, research and development, and workforce training will drive long-term economic growth and competitiveness.

- **Incentivizing Infrastructure Investment:** Providing tax incentives for businesses that invest in infrastructure projects, such as transportation, energy, and digital infrastructure. This includes offering tax credits and deductions for investments that create jobs and stimulate economic activity.

- **Supporting Research and Development:** Implementing tax incentives for businesses that invest in research and development activities. This includes expanding the R&D tax credit and providing support for innovation and technological advancements.

- **Encouraging Workforce Training:** Offering tax incentives for businesses that invest in workforce training and development programs. This includes providing support for apprenticeship programs, vocational training, and continuing education initiatives.

4. Supporting Small Businesses

Supporting small businesses is a critical aspect of the Trump-Vance tax reform plan. They recognize that small businesses are the backbone of the American economy and are essential for job creation and economic growth.

- **Reducing the Tax Burden on Small Businesses:** Implementing measures to reduce the tax burden on small businesses, making it easier for them to operate and grow. This includes lowering tax rates for small businesses and providing targeted tax relief for startups and entrepreneurs.

- **Expanding Access to Capital:** Providing tax incentives and support for small businesses to access capital and financing. This includes expanding loan programs, grants, and tax credits for small businesses that invest in growth and expansion.

- **Promoting Entrepreneurship:** Encouraging entrepreneurship through tax incentives and support for startups. This includes providing resources and support for new business ventures, particularly those in underrepresented communities.

Regulatory Relief

Reducing regulatory burdens is another key component of the Trump-Vance economic agenda. They believe that excessive regulations stifle innovation, increase costs, and hinder economic growth. Their regulatory relief proposals aim to create a more business-friendly environment that fosters innovation and entrepreneurship.

1. Streamlining Regulations

Streamlining regulations is essential for reducing the administrative burden on businesses and promoting economic growth. The Trump-Vance regulatory relief plan includes measures to simplify and consolidate regulations, making it easier for businesses to comply with regulatory requirements.

- **Reducing Red Tape:** Implementing measures to reduce red tape and streamline regulatory processes. This includes eliminating redundant and outdated regulations and consolidating regulatory agencies to improve efficiency.

- **Improving Regulatory Transparency:** Enhancing regulatory transparency by providing clear and accessible information about regulatory requirements. This includes creating online portals and resources to help businesses navigate the regulatory landscape.

2. Reducing Compliance Costs

Reducing compliance costs is essential for making it easier for businesses to operate and grow. The Trump-Vance regulatory relief plan includes measures to reduce the cost of compliance and ensure that businesses can focus on innovation and growth.

- **Implementing Cost-Benefit Analysis:** Requiring regulatory agencies to conduct cost-benefit analyses of proposed regulations to ensure that they provide net benefits to the economy. This includes evaluating the economic impact of regulations and considering alternative approaches.

- **Promoting Flexibility:** Implementing measures to promote flexibility in regulatory compliance, allowing businesses to choose the most effective and efficient methods for meeting regulatory requirements. This includes providing options for businesses to demonstrate compliance through performance-based standards.

3. Supporting Innovation and Entrepreneurship

Supporting innovation and entrepreneurship is essential for driving economic growth and competitiveness. The Trump-Vance regulatory relief plan includes measures to promote innovation and create a more conducive environment for startups and small businesses.

- **Encouraging Regulatory Experimentation:** Implementing measures to encourage regulatory experimentation and innovation. This includes creating regulatory sandboxes that allow businesses to test new products and services in a controlled environment with reduced regulatory oversight.

- **Promoting Public-Private Partnerships:** Encouraging collaboration between the public and private sectors to develop innovative regulatory solutions. This includes supporting initiatives that bring together businesses, government agencies, and academic institutions to address regulatory challenges.

Infrastructure Investment

Investing in infrastructure is a key component of the Trump-Vance economic agenda. They recognize that modern, efficient infrastructure is critical for economic growth and competitiveness. Their infrastructure investment proposals include significant funding for transportation, energy, and digital infrastructure projects.

1. Transportation Infrastructure

Investing in transportation infrastructure is essential for improving connectivity, reducing congestion, and enhancing safety. The Trump-Vance infrastructure investment plan includes measures to modernize and expand transportation infrastructure, including roads, bridges, airports, and public transit systems.

- **Funding for Roads and Bridges:** Increasing funding for the construction and maintenance of roads and bridges. This includes investing in projects that enhance connectivity, reduce traffic congestion, and improve safety.

- **Expanding Public Transit:** Supporting the expansion of public transit systems to provide affordable and efficient transportation options. This includes funding for the development of new transit lines, upgrading existing systems, and promoting multimodal transportation solutions.

- **Improving Airport Infrastructure:** Investing in the modernization and expansion of airport infrastructure to enhance the efficiency and capacity of air travel. This includes funding for terminal upgrades, runway improvements, and the development of new airports.

2. Energy Infrastructure

Investing in energy infrastructure is essential for promoting energy security and supporting the transition to a clean energy economy. The Trump-Vance infrastructure investment plan includes measures to develop and deploy clean energy technologies, expand the electric grid, and enhance energy efficiency.

- **Promoting Clean Energy Development:** Increasing funding for the development and deployment of clean energy technologies, such as wind, solar, and hydropower. This includes providing tax incentives and grants for clean energy projects and supporting research and development in renewable energy.

- **Expanding the Electric Grid:** Investing in the expansion and modernization of the electric grid to enhance reliability and support the integration of renewable energy sources. This includes funding for grid infrastructure projects, such as transmission lines and energy storage systems.

- **Enhancing Energy Efficiency:** Implementing measures to promote energy efficiency and reduce energy consumption. This includes providing incentives for businesses and households to adopt energy-efficient technologies and practices.

3. Digital Infrastructure

Investing in digital infrastructure is essential for supporting innovation, enhancing connectivity, and promoting economic growth. The Trump-Vance infrastructure investment plan includes measures to expand broadband internet access, develop 5G networks, and promote digital literacy and inclusion.

- **Expanding Broadband Access:** Increasing funding for the expansion of broadband internet access to underserved and rural areas. This includes providing grants and loans to support the deployment of high-speed internet infrastructure and promoting initiatives that enhance digital connectivity.

- **Developing 5G Networks:** Supporting the development and deployment of 5G networks to enhance connectivity and support the next generation of digital technologies. This includes funding for the construction of 5G infrastructure and promoting public-private partnerships to accelerate the rollout of 5G services.

- **Promoting Digital Literacy and Inclusion:** Implementing measures to promote digital literacy and inclusion, ensuring that all Americans have the skills and resources they need to participate in the digital economy. This includes funding for digital literacy programs, providing support for low-income households to access digital devices, and promoting initiatives that bridge the digital divide.

Support for Small Businesses

Supporting small businesses is a critical aspect of the Trump-Vance economic agenda. They recognize that small businesses are the backbone of the American economy and are essential for job creation and economic growth. Their policies aim to create a more supportive environment for small businesses and ensure that they have the resources and opportunities they need to succeed.

1. Access to Capital

Increasing access to capital is essential for helping small businesses grow and thrive. The Trump-Vance economic agenda includes measures to expand loan programs, grants, and tax incentives for small businesses that invest in growth and expansion.

- **Expanding Loan Programs:** Increasing funding for loan programs that provide financing to small businesses. This includes supporting initiatives such as the Small Business Administration (SBA) loan programs, which provide low-interest loans to small businesses for working capital, equipment purchases, and expansion projects.

- **Providing Grants and Tax Incentives:** Implementing measures to provide grants and tax incentives for small businesses that invest in growth and expansion. This includes offering tax credits for businesses that create jobs, invest in research and development, and support workforce training programs.

2. Reducing Regulatory Burdens

Reducing regulatory burdens is essential for making it easier for small businesses to operate and grow. The Trump-Vance economic agenda includes measures to streamline regulations, reduce compliance costs, and provide resources and support to help small businesses navigate regulatory requirements.

- **Streamlining Regulations:** Implementing measures to streamline regulations and reduce the administrative burden on small businesses. This includes eliminating redundant and outdated regulations, consolidating regulatory agencies, and providing clear and accessible information about regulatory requirements.

- **Reducing Compliance Costs:** Implementing measures to reduce compliance costs and ensure that small businesses can focus on innovation and growth. This includes promoting flexibility in regulatory compliance, allowing businesses to choose the most effective and efficient methods for meeting regulatory requirements.

3. Promoting Entrepreneurship

Promoting entrepreneurship is essential for driving economic growth and innovation. The Trump-Vance economic agenda includes measures to support startups and new business ventures, particularly those in underrepresented communities.

- **Supporting Entrepreneurship Education:** Increasing funding for entrepreneurship education programs that provide training, mentorship, and support for aspiring business owners. This includes funding for programs that promote entrepreneurship in schools, colleges, and community organizations.

- **Encouraging Innovation and Startups:** Implementing measures to encourage innovation and support startups. This includes providing resources and support for new business ventures, creating regulatory sandboxes that allow businesses to test new products and services in a controlled environment, and promoting public-private partnerships to develop innovative solutions.

Promoting Economic Opportunity

Promoting economic opportunity is a key priority of the Trump-Vance economic agenda. They believe that ensuring all Americans have access to economic opportunities is essential for creating a more just and equitable society. Their policies focus on addressing economic disparities, supporting workforce development, and promoting job creation.

1. Addressing Economic Disparities

Addressing economic disparities is essential for promoting social justice and ensuring that all Americans have the opportunity to succeed. The Trump-Vance economic agenda includes measures to address economic disparities and promote economic opportunity for all.

- **Supporting Low-Income Communities:** Implementing measures to support low-income communities and promote economic development. This includes increasing funding for community development programs, providing support for affordable housing initiatives, and promoting economic opportunity in underserved areas.

- **Promoting Workforce Diversity:** Implementing measures to promote workforce diversity and ensure that all individuals have access to economic opportunities. This includes supporting initiatives that promote diversity in hiring, providing resources and support for minority-owned businesses, and implementing measures to address discrimination in the workplace.

2. Supporting Workforce Development

Supporting workforce development is essential for ensuring that all Americans have the skills and opportunities they need to succeed in the modern economy. The Trump-Vance economic agenda includes measures to support workforce training, education, and development programs.

- **Expanding Workforce Training Programs:** Increasing funding for workforce training programs that provide individuals with the skills and training they need to succeed in the modern economy. This includes supporting apprenticeship programs, vocational training, and continuing education initiatives.

- **Promoting Career and Technical Education:** Supporting career and technical education programs that provide students with practical skills and training. This includes increasing funding for career and technical education programs, promoting dual enrollment programs, and providing support for students who pursue career and technical education.

3. Creating Jobs and Promoting Economic Growth

Creating jobs and promoting economic growth is essential for ensuring that all Americans have access to economic opportunities. The Trump-Vance economic agenda includes measures to promote job creation, support small businesses, and stimulate economic activity.

- **Investing in Infrastructure Projects:** Investing in infrastructure projects that create jobs and stimulate economic growth. This includes funding for transportation, energy, and digital infrastructure projects that provide employment opportunities and improve the overall competitiveness of the economy.

- **Supporting Small Business Growth:** Implementing measures to support small business growth and promote entrepreneurship. This includes providing access to capital, reducing regulatory burdens, and promoting initiatives that support small business development.

Conclusion

The Trump-Vance approach to tax reform and economic policy represents a bold and comprehensive strategy for promoting economic growth and prosperity. Their policies are designed to address the underlying structural issues that contribute to economic inequality and stagnation and ensure that the benefits of prosperity are broadly shared.

By focusing on tax reform, regulatory relief, infrastructure investment, and support for small businesses, the Trump-Vance campaign aims to create a more vibrant and equitable economy. Their commitment to promoting economic opportunity and supporting the working class offers a pathway to renewed prosperity and opportunity for all Americans.

As we continue to explore the specific policies and initiatives proposed by the Trump-Vance partnership, it is clear that their vision for the future of the United States is grounded in the principles of economic nationalism, job creation, and support for the working class. Their commitment to promoting economic growth and prosperity offers a pathway to a brighter and more inclusive future for all Americans.

In the next chapter, we will explore their strategies for immigration policy and border security, providing a comprehensive understanding of their approach to addressing these critical issues. Join us as we continue to explore the dynamic and impactful partnership of Donald Trump and J.D. Vance, and discover how their combined efforts could reshape the future of American politics and society.

Chapter 8: Immigration Policy and Border Security

Immigration policy and border security are critical issues that significantly impact the social, economic, and political landscape of the United States. The Trump-Vance campaign has developed a comprehensive approach to addressing these challenges, focusing on securing the borders, reforming the immigration system, and promoting legal immigration. This chapter delves into their strategies and policies, exploring their vision for a more secure and orderly immigration system.

The State of Immigration in America

The United States has long been a destination for immigrants seeking better opportunities and a chance at the American Dream. However, the country has faced significant challenges in managing immigration, balancing the needs of national security, economic growth, and humanitarian concerns. Issues such as illegal immigration, border security, and the complexities of the legal immigration system have sparked intense debate and policy discussions.

Illegal immigration remains a contentious issue, with concerns about its impact on jobs, public resources, and national security. At the same time, the legal immigration system is often criticized for being overly complex, slow, and inefficient. Addressing these issues requires a multifaceted approach that ensures the security of the borders, promotes legal immigration, and provides a fair and humane treatment of immigrants.

The Trump-Vance Immigration Vision

The Trump-Vance vision for immigration policy is centered on the principles of national security, rule of law, and economic opportunity. Their policies are designed to secure the borders, enforce immigration laws, and create a more efficient and fair legal immigration system. Key components of their immigration agenda include border security, reforming the legal immigration system, addressing illegal immigration, and promoting integration and assimilation.

Border Security

Securing the borders is a top priority for the Trump-Vance campaign. They believe that a secure border is essential for protecting the sovereignty of the United States and preventing the entry of illegal immigrants, drugs, and other threats. Their approach to border security includes a combination of physical barriers, technological solutions, and enhanced enforcement measures.

1. Building Physical Barriers

Constructing physical barriers, such as walls and fences, is a key component of the Trump-Vance border security strategy. They believe that physical barriers are an effective way to prevent illegal crossings and enhance the overall security of the border.

- **Continuing the Border Wall Construction:** Completing the construction of the border wall along the U.S.-Mexico border to prevent illegal crossings. This includes funding for new sections of the wall, as well as repairs and upgrades to existing barriers.

- **Improving Existing Barriers:** Enhancing the effectiveness of existing barriers by upgrading and maintaining fences, walls, and other physical structures. This includes implementing measures to address vulnerabilities and ensure that barriers provide effective deterrence.

2. Implementing Technological Solutions

Utilizing advanced technologies to enhance border security is another critical element of the Trump-Vance strategy. This includes deploying surveillance systems, drones, and sensors to monitor the border and detect illegal activity.

- **Deploying Surveillance Systems:** Implementing advanced surveillance systems, such as cameras, sensors, and radar, to monitor the border and detect illegal crossings. This includes funding for the deployment and maintenance of these systems.

- **Using Drones and Aerial Surveillance:** Utilizing drones and other aerial surveillance technologies to provide real-time monitoring of the border. This includes funding for the acquisition and operation of drones and other aerial platforms.

- **Implementing Biometric Technologies:** Enhancing border security through the use of biometric technologies, such as facial recognition and fingerprint scanning. This includes funding for the development and deployment of biometric systems to improve the identification and tracking of individuals entering and exiting the country.

3. Enhancing Border Enforcement

Increasing funding and resources for border enforcement agencies, such as U.S. Customs and Border Protection (CBP) and Immigration and Customs Enforcement (ICE), is essential for ensuring effective border security.

- **Hiring Additional Agents:** Increasing the number of border patrol agents and immigration enforcement officers to enhance border security and enforce immigration laws. This includes funding for recruitment, training, and equipment for new personnel.

- **Improving Training and Resources:** Providing advanced training and resources for border enforcement personnel to ensure that they are equipped to handle a wide range of challenges. This includes funding for specialized training programs, equipment, and technology.

- **Enhancing Coordination and Collaboration:** Improving coordination and collaboration between federal, state, and local law enforcement agencies to enhance border security efforts. This includes funding for joint operations, information sharing, and interagency cooperation.

Reforming the Legal Immigration System

Reforming the legal immigration system is a critical aspect of the Trump-Vance immigration agenda. They believe that creating a more efficient and fair legal immigration system is essential for promoting economic growth, ensuring national security, and upholding the rule of law.

1. Streamlining the Immigration Process

Simplifying and streamlining the legal immigration process is essential for reducing backlogs and ensuring that individuals can enter the country legally and efficiently.

- **Reducing Application Backlogs:** Implementing measures to reduce backlogs in the immigration application process. This includes increasing funding for immigration processing centers, hiring additional staff, and improving technology and infrastructure.

- **Simplifying the Application Process:** Simplifying the immigration application process to make it more straightforward and user-friendly. This includes reducing paperwork, providing clear and accessible information, and implementing online application systems.

- **Enhancing Processing Times:** Implementing measures to enhance processing times for immigration applications. This includes setting performance targets, improving workflow management, and utilizing technology to streamline processing.

2. Promoting Skilled Immigration

Promoting skilled immigration is essential for ensuring that the United States remains competitive in the global economy. The Trump-Vance immigration agenda includes measures to attract and retain highly skilled immigrants.

- **Expanding Visa Programs for Skilled Workers:** Increasing the number of visas available for skilled workers, such as H-1B visas. This includes implementing measures to prioritize visas for individuals with advanced degrees and specialized skills.

- **Providing Pathways to Permanent Residency:** Creating pathways to permanent residency for skilled workers who contribute to the economy. This includes implementing measures to facilitate the transition from temporary work visas to permanent residency.

- **Supporting International Students:** Encouraging international students to study in the United States and remain in the country after graduation. This includes providing incentives for students to pursue degrees in STEM fields and offering pathways to permanent residency for graduates.

3. Promoting Family Reunification

Promoting family reunification is a key aspect of the Trump-Vance immigration agenda. They believe that keeping families together is essential for social stability and cohesion.

- **Expanding Family-Based Visa Programs:** Increasing the number of visas available for family reunification. This includes implementing measures to prioritize visas for immediate family members, such as spouses and children.

- **Reducing Wait Times for Family Reunification:** Implementing measures to reduce wait times for family-based immigration applications. This includes increasing funding for processing centers, improving technology and infrastructure, and setting performance targets for processing times.

- **Supporting Family Reunification Programs:** Providing support and resources for family reunification programs. This includes funding for organizations that assist with family reunification, providing legal assistance, and offering support services for families.

Addressing Illegal Immigration

Addressing illegal immigration is a critical component of the Trump-Vance immigration agenda. They believe that enforcing immigration laws and promoting legal immigration is essential for ensuring national security and upholding the rule of law.

1. Enforcing Immigration Laws

Enforcing immigration laws is essential for deterring illegal immigration and ensuring that individuals who violate immigration laws are held accountable.

- **Enhancing Interior Enforcement:** Increasing funding and resources for interior enforcement efforts, such as those conducted by ICE. This includes hiring additional enforcement officers, improving technology and infrastructure, and enhancing coordination with state and local law enforcement agencies.

- **Implementing E-Verify:** Expanding the use of E-Verify to ensure that employers verify the legal status of their employees. This includes making E-Verify mandatory for all employers and providing support for businesses to implement the system.

- **Addressing Visa Overstays:** Implementing measures to address visa overstays, which are a significant source of illegal immigration. This includes enhancing tracking and enforcement efforts and providing support for individuals to comply with visa requirements.

2. Promoting Legal Immigration

Promoting legal immigration is essential for ensuring that individuals have a clear and accessible pathway to enter the country legally.

- **Providing Clear Pathways to Legal Status:** Creating clear and accessible pathways to legal status for individuals who meet specific criteria. This includes implementing measures to streamline the application process and provide support for individuals seeking legal status.

- **Encouraging Voluntary Compliance:** Implementing measures to encourage voluntary compliance with immigration laws. This includes providing incentives for individuals to come forward and regularize their status and offering support for individuals who seek to comply with immigration laws.

- **Supporting Immigration Education and Outreach:** Providing education and outreach to individuals and communities about the legal immigration process. This includes funding for programs that provide information and resources about immigration laws and the legal immigration process.

3. Addressing the Root Causes of Illegal Immigration

Addressing the root causes of illegal immigration is essential for creating long-term solutions to the challenges of illegal immigration. The Trump-Vance immigration agenda includes measures to address the factors that drive individuals to migrate illegally.

- **Promoting Economic Development in Source Countries:** Supporting economic development initiatives in countries that are significant sources of illegal immigration. This includes funding for programs that promote job creation, education, and infrastructure development in these countries.

- **Enhancing Security and Stability:** Implementing measures to enhance security and stability in source countries. This includes providing support for law enforcement and security initiatives, promoting political stability, and addressing issues such as violence and corruption.

- **Supporting International Cooperation:** Promoting international cooperation to address the root causes of illegal immigration. This includes working with international organizations, foreign governments, and non-governmental organizations to develop coordinated responses to the challenges of illegal immigration.

Promoting Integration and Assimilation

Promoting the integration and assimilation of immigrants is essential for ensuring that they can contribute to society and achieve their full potential. The Trump-Vance immigration agenda includes measures to support the successful integration and assimilation of immigrants into American society.

1. Providing Support for New Immigrants

Providing support for new immigrants is essential for helping them navigate the challenges of settling in a new country. The Trump-Vance immigration agenda includes measures to provide support and resources for new immigrants.

- **Offering Language and Education Programs:** Increasing funding for language and education programs that help new immigrants learn English and acquire essential skills. This includes funding for English as a Second Language (ESL) programs, adult education classes, and vocational training.

- **Providing Legal Assistance:** Offering legal assistance and support for new immigrants to help them navigate the immigration system. This includes funding for legal aid organizations, providing information and resources about immigration laws, and offering assistance with legal paperwork and applications.

- **Supporting Community Integration Programs:** Implementing programs that support the integration of new immigrants into their communities. This includes funding for community centers, social services, and cultural programs that promote community engagement and integration.

2. Promoting Civic Engagement

Promoting civic engagement is essential for ensuring that immigrants are active and engaged members of society. The Trump-Vance immigration agenda includes measures to encourage civic participation and promote a sense of belonging and community.

- **Encouraging Naturalization:** Promoting naturalization and citizenship for immigrants who meet the eligibility criteria. This includes providing support for the naturalization process, offering citizenship education programs, and encouraging eligible immigrants to apply for citizenship.

- **Supporting Civic Education:** Implementing civic education programs that provide immigrants with information about their rights and responsibilities as citizens. This includes funding for programs that teach immigrants about the political system, civic engagement, and community participation.

- **Promoting Volunteerism and Community Service:** Encouraging immigrants to participate in volunteerism and community service activities. This includes funding for programs that promote volunteer opportunities, supporting community service initiatives, and recognizing the contributions of immigrants to their communities.

3. Addressing Discrimination and Bias

Addressing discrimination and bias is essential for ensuring that immigrants are treated fairly and have equal opportunities to succeed. The Trump-Vance immigration agenda includes measures to promote diversity and inclusion and address issues of discrimination and bias.

- **Promoting Anti-Discrimination Policies:** Implementing and enforcing anti-discrimination policies that protect immigrants from discrimination and bias. This includes increasing funding for enforcement of anti-discrimination laws, providing support for individuals who experience discrimination, and promoting diversity and inclusion initiatives.

- **Supporting Cultural Competency Training:** Providing cultural competency training for government officials, law enforcement, and service providers to ensure that they are equipped to work with diverse populations. This includes funding for training programs, promoting best practices in cultural competency, and encouraging diversity in the workforce.

- **Raising Awareness and Promoting Inclusion:** Implementing public awareness campaigns that promote diversity, inclusion, and respect for all individuals. This includes funding for initiatives that raise awareness about the contributions of immigrants, promote understanding and acceptance, and address issues of bias and discrimination.

Conclusion

The Trump-Vance approach to immigration policy and border security represents a comprehensive and multifaceted strategy for addressing the challenges of immigration and promoting national security. Their policies are designed to secure the borders, enforce immigration laws, and create a more efficient and fair legal immigration system.

By focusing on border security, reforming the legal immigration system, addressing illegal immigration, and promoting integration and assimilation, the Trump-Vance campaign aims to create a more secure and orderly immigration system. Their commitment to promoting legal immigration and supporting the successful integration of immigrants offers a pathway to a brighter and more inclusive future for all Americans.

As we continue to explore the specific policies and initiatives proposed by the Trump-Vance partnership, it is clear that their vision for the future of the United States is grounded in the principles of national security, rule of law, and economic opportunity. Their commitment to addressing the challenges of immigration and promoting a secure and orderly immigration system offers a pathway to a more secure and prosperous future for all Americans.

In the next chapter, we will explore their strategies for education reform, providing a comprehensive understanding of their approach to addressing the critical issues in the education system. Join us as we continue to explore the dynamic and impactful partnership of Donald Trump and J.D. Vance, and discover how their combined efforts could reshape the future of American politics and society.

A Hillbilly Elegy for America

Chapter 9: Education Reform

Education is a fundamental pillar of society and a critical factor in promoting economic opportunity, social mobility, and national competitiveness. The Trump-Vance campaign recognizes the importance of addressing the challenges facing the U.S. education system and has developed a comprehensive approach to education reform. This chapter delves into their strategies and policies, exploring their vision for improving educational outcomes and ensuring that all Americans have access to quality education.

The State of Education in America

The American education system faces numerous challenges, including disparities in funding and resources, achievement gaps, and varying levels of access to quality education. These challenges are particularly pronounced in low-income and minority communities, where students often face significant barriers to academic success.

Funding disparities between school districts, outdated curricula, and a lack of support for teachers contribute to inconsistent educational outcomes. Additionally, the COVID-19 pandemic has exacerbated existing inequalities, highlighting the urgent need for comprehensive education reform.

The Trump-Vance Education Vision

The education vision of Donald Trump and J.D. Vance is centered on the principles of equality, excellence, and innovation. Their policies are designed to address the root causes of educational disparities, support teachers, and promote student achievement. Key components of their education agenda include increasing funding for schools, promoting school choice, supporting teachers, and modernizing the curriculum.

Increasing Funding for Schools

Adequate funding is essential for ensuring that all students have access to quality education. The Trump-Vance education agenda includes measures to increase funding for schools, particularly those in low-income areas, and to ensure that resources are allocated equitably.

1. Addressing Funding Disparities

Addressing funding disparities between school districts is critical for promoting educational equity. The Trump-Vance campaign proposes measures to ensure that all schools receive adequate funding, regardless of their location or the socioeconomic status of their students.

- **Implementing Equitable Funding Formulas:** Developing and implementing funding formulas that allocate resources based on the needs of students and schools. This includes providing additional funding for schools that serve low-income communities, students with disabilities, and English language learners.

- **Increasing Federal Funding for Education:** Increasing federal funding for education to support state and local efforts to address funding disparities. This includes expanding programs such as Title I, which provides financial assistance to schools with high numbers of low-income students.

- **Supporting Infrastructure Improvements:** Providing funding for infrastructure improvements to ensure that all schools have safe and modern facilities. This includes funding for the renovation and construction of school buildings, as well as investments in technology and resources.

2. Expanding Access to Early Childhood Education

Early childhood education is a critical factor in promoting long-term academic success and social development. The Trump-Vance education agenda includes measures to expand access to early childhood education programs and ensure that all children have the opportunity to start school ready to learn.

- **Increasing Funding for Preschool Programs:** Increasing funding for preschool programs to ensure that all children have access to high-quality early childhood education. This includes expanding programs such as Head Start and providing support for state and local preschool initiatives.

- **Supporting Universal Pre-K:** Implementing measures to support the development of universal pre-kindergarten programs. This includes providing funding for universal pre-K initiatives and promoting partnerships between public and private providers.

- **Promoting Early Childhood Education Research:** Supporting research and innovation in early childhood education to identify effective practices and improve program quality. This includes funding for studies on early childhood development and education, as well as initiatives to disseminate best practices.

Promoting School Choice

School choice is a key aspect of the Trump-Vance education agenda. They believe that providing families with a range of educational options is essential for promoting competition, innovation, and improved educational outcomes.

1. Expanding Charter Schools

Charter schools are publicly funded schools that operate independently of traditional school district regulations. The Trump-Vance campaign supports the expansion of charter schools as a means of providing families with more educational options.

- **Increasing Funding for Charter Schools:** Providing additional funding to support the development and expansion of charter schools. This includes funding for new charter school startups, facilities, and innovative programs.

- **Promoting Accountability and Transparency:** Ensuring that charter schools are held to high standards of accountability and transparency. This includes implementing measures to monitor the performance of charter schools and ensure that they provide a high-quality education to all students.

- **Encouraging Innovation in Charter Schools:** Promoting innovation in charter schools by supporting initiatives that develop and implement new educational models and practices. This includes funding for research and pilot programs that explore innovative approaches to teaching and learning.

2. Supporting Voucher Programs

Voucher programs provide families with financial assistance to send their children to private schools of their choice. The Trump-Vance education agenda includes measures to expand voucher programs and provide families with greater access to private education.

- **Expanding Voucher Programs:** Increasing funding for voucher programs to ensure that more families have access to private education. This includes providing additional vouchers for low-income families and students with disabilities.

- **Ensuring Equity in Voucher Programs:** Implementing measures to ensure that voucher programs are equitable and do not exacerbate existing disparities. This includes providing support for families to navigate the voucher application process and ensuring that voucher programs are available to all students.

- **Promoting Accountability in Private Schools:** Ensuring that private schools that participate in voucher programs are held to high standards of accountability. This includes implementing measures to monitor the performance of private schools and ensure that they provide a high-quality education to all students.

3. Supporting Homeschooling and Alternative Education

Homeschooling and alternative education options provide families with additional flexibility and choice in their children's education. The Trump-Vance education agenda includes measures to support homeschooling and alternative education models.

- **Providing Resources for Homeschooling Families:** Offering resources and support for families who choose to homeschool their children. This includes funding for curriculum materials, online courses, and extracurricular activities.

- **Supporting Alternative Education Models:** Promoting the development and expansion of alternative education models, such as online schools, micro-schools, and community-based education programs. This includes funding for pilot programs and research on alternative education practices.

- **Ensuring Flexibility in Education Policy:** Implementing measures to ensure that education policies provide flexibility for families to choose the best educational options for their children. This includes promoting policies that allow for personalized learning and student-centered approaches.

Supporting Teachers

Teachers play a critical role in promoting student achievement and ensuring that all students have access to quality education. The Trump-Vance education agenda includes measures to support teachers and ensure that they have the resources and training they need to succeed.

1. Increasing Teacher Salaries

Ensuring that teachers are fairly compensated for their work is essential for attracting and retaining high-quality educators. The Trump-Vance campaign proposes measures to increase teacher salaries and provide financial incentives for teachers in high-need areas.

- **Increasing Base Salaries for Teachers:** Implementing measures to increase base salaries for teachers, ensuring that they receive fair compensation for their work. This includes providing additional funding for teacher salaries at the state and local levels.

- **Providing Incentives for High-Need Areas:** Offering financial incentives for teachers who work in high-need areas, such as low-income schools and rural communities. This includes providing bonuses, housing assistance, and other forms of support.

- **Supporting Teacher Loan Forgiveness Programs:** Expanding teacher loan forgiveness programs to reduce the financial burden on educators. This includes providing additional funding for loan forgiveness programs and promoting initiatives that support teachers in repaying their student loans.

2. Enhancing Professional Development

Providing opportunities for professional development is essential for ensuring that teachers have the skills and knowledge they need to succeed. The Trump-Vance education agenda includes measures to enhance professional development for teachers and promote ongoing learning and growth.

- **Increasing Funding for Professional Development:** Providing additional funding for professional development programs that support teacher growth and development. This includes funding for workshops, conferences, and continuing education courses.

- **Supporting Mentorship Programs:** Implementing mentorship programs that provide support and guidance for new and experienced teachers. This includes funding for mentorship initiatives, training for mentor teachers, and resources for mentees.

- **Promoting Collaborative Learning:** Encouraging collaborative learning and professional development among teachers. This includes supporting initiatives that promote peer observation, team teaching, and professional learning communities.

3. Improving Teacher Working Conditions

Ensuring that teachers have positive working conditions is essential for promoting job satisfaction and retention. The Trump-Vance education agenda includes measures to improve teacher working conditions and address issues such as burnout and turnover.

- **Reducing Class Sizes:** Implementing measures to reduce class sizes and ensure that teachers can provide individualized attention to their students. This includes funding for additional teachers and classroom resources.

- **Providing Adequate Resources:** Ensuring that teachers have access to the resources and materials they need to succeed. This includes funding for classroom supplies, technology, and instructional materials.

- **Addressing Teacher Burnout:** Implementing measures to address teacher burnout and promote well-being. This includes providing support for mental health and wellness programs, promoting work-life balance, and offering opportunities for stress management and self-care.

Modernizing the Curriculum

Modernizing the curriculum is essential for ensuring that students are prepared for the demands of the modern economy and society. The Trump-Vance education agenda includes measures to update and enhance the curriculum, promote STEM education, and support career and technical education.

1. Updating and Enhancing the Curriculum

Updating and enhancing the curriculum is essential for providing students with a well-rounded and relevant education. The Trump-Vance campaign proposes measures to modernize the curriculum and ensure that it reflects current knowledge and skills.

- **Incorporating Modern Topics and Skills:** Implementing measures to incorporate modern topics and skills into the curriculum, such as digital literacy, financial literacy, and critical thinking. This includes updating standards and guidelines to reflect current knowledge and best practices.

- **Promoting Culturally Relevant Curriculum:** Ensuring that the curriculum is culturally relevant and inclusive. This includes incorporating diverse perspectives and experiences into the curriculum and promoting initiatives that support culturally responsive teaching.

- **Supporting Curriculum Innovation:** Encouraging innovation in curriculum development and implementation. This includes funding for research and pilot programs that explore new approaches to teaching and learning.

2. Promoting STEM Education

Promoting STEM (science, technology, engineering, and mathematics) education is essential for preparing students for the demands of the modern economy. The Trump-Vance education agenda includes measures to enhance STEM education and ensure that all students have access to high-quality STEM programs.

- **Increasing Funding for STEM Programs:** Providing additional funding for STEM education programs at all levels of education. This includes funding for STEM curriculum development, teacher training, and student engagement initiatives.

- **Supporting STEM Teacher Development:** Implementing measures to support the development of STEM teachers. This includes funding for professional development programs, mentorship initiatives, and incentives for teachers who specialize in STEM subjects.

- **Encouraging Student Participation in STEM:** Promoting initiatives that encourage student participation in STEM education. This includes funding for extracurricular STEM activities, competitions, and partnerships with industry and higher education institutions.

3. Supporting Career and Technical Education

Supporting career and technical education (CTE) is essential for providing students with the skills and training they need to succeed in the workforce. The Trump-Vance education agenda includes measures to enhance CTE programs and ensure that students have access to high-quality vocational training.

- **Expanding Access to CTE Programs:** Increasing funding for CTE programs to ensure that all students have access to high-quality vocational training. This includes funding for CTE curriculum development, facilities, and equipment.

- **Promoting Partnerships with Industry:** Encouraging partnerships between CTE programs and industry to provide students with real-world experience and training. This includes funding for apprenticeship programs, internships, and industry collaborations.

- **Supporting CTE Teacher Development:** Implementing measures to support the development of CTE teachers. This includes funding for professional development programs, mentorship initiatives, and incentives for teachers who specialize in CTE subjects.

Conclusion

The Trump-Vance approach to education reform represents a bold and comprehensive strategy for improving educational outcomes and ensuring that all Americans have access to quality education. Their policies are designed to address the root causes of educational disparities, support teachers, and promote student achievement.

By focusing on increasing funding for schools, promoting school choice, supporting teachers, and modernizing the curriculum, the Trump-Vance campaign aims to create a more equitable and effective education system. Their commitment to promoting educational excellence and opportunity offers a pathway to a brighter and more inclusive future for all Americans.

As we continue to explore the specific policies and initiatives proposed by the Trump-Vance partnership, it is clear that their vision for the future of the United States is grounded in the principles of equality, excellence, and innovation. Their commitment to addressing the challenges facing the education system and promoting student success offers a pathway to a more prosperous and competitive future for all Americans.

In the next chapter, we will explore their strategies for healthcare reform, providing a comprehensive understanding of their approach to addressing the critical issues in the healthcare system. Join us as we continue to explore the dynamic and impactful partnership of Donald Trump and J.D. Vance, and discover how their combined efforts could reshape the future of American politics and society.

Conclusion

The partnership between Donald Trump and J.D. Vance represents a dynamic and innovative approach to addressing the critical issues facing the United States today. Their comprehensive policy agenda is designed to promote economic growth, social justice, national security, and educational excellence, reflecting a deep commitment to revitalizing the American Dream and ensuring that all Americans have the opportunity to succeed.

Reclaiming Economic Prosperity

At the core of the Trump-Vance agenda is a commitment to reclaiming economic prosperity for all Americans. Their economic policies are focused on stimulating growth, creating jobs, and ensuring that the benefits of economic success are widely shared. Through tax reform, regulatory relief, and significant investments in infrastructure and small businesses, they aim to create a vibrant and inclusive economy.

- **Tax Reform:** By reducing corporate tax rates, simplifying the tax code, and promoting investment and job creation, the Trump-Vance tax reform plan seeks to make American businesses more competitive globally and ensure that individuals and families benefit from economic growth.

- **Regulatory Relief:** Reducing regulatory burdens on businesses, particularly small businesses, is essential for fostering innovation and entrepreneurship. The Trump-Vance agenda includes measures to streamline regulations, reduce compliance costs, and promote public-private partnerships.

- **Infrastructure Investment:** Investing in transportation, energy, and digital infrastructure is critical for supporting economic growth and competitiveness. The Trump-Vance plan includes significant funding for infrastructure projects that create jobs and stimulate economic activity.

- **Supporting Small Businesses:** Small businesses are the backbone of the American economy, and the Trump-Vance agenda includes measures to increase access to capital, reduce regulatory burdens, and promote entrepreneurship and innovation.

Promoting Social Justice and Equality

Social justice and equality are foundational principles of the Trump-Vance vision for America's future. Their policies are designed to address disparities in income, education, healthcare, and criminal justice, ensuring that all Americans have the opportunity to achieve their full potential.

- **Economic Equality and Opportunity:** Addressing income inequality, supporting small businesses, and promoting job creation and workforce development are key priorities of the Trump-Vance agenda. Their policies aim to ensure that all Americans have access to economic opportunities and can achieve economic success.

- **Education Reform:** Improving educational outcomes and ensuring access to quality education for all students is essential for promoting social mobility and economic opportunity. The Trump-Vance education agenda includes measures to increase funding for schools, promote school choice, support teachers, and modernize the curriculum.

- **Healthcare Access and Equity:** Ensuring access to affordable and comprehensive healthcare is a critical aspect of the Trump-Vance vision for social justice. Their healthcare policies include measures to expand coverage, reduce costs, and enhance the quality of care, ensuring that all Americans have access to the healthcare services they need.

- **Criminal Justice Reform:** Promoting fairness in the criminal justice system and reducing mass incarceration are key priorities of the Trump-Vance agenda. Their policies include measures to address sentencing disparities, expand alternatives to incarceration, and support reentry programs for individuals transitioning back into society.

Ensuring National Security and Border Security

National security and border security are critical components of the Trump-Vance vision for America's future. Their policies are designed to ensure the safety and security of the American people, maintain a strong national defense, and promote a secure and orderly immigration system.

- **Strengthening the Military:** Maintaining a strong and capable military is essential for protecting the sovereignty and interests of the United States. The Trump-Vance defense strategy includes increasing defense spending, modernizing the military, enhancing readiness and capabilities, and supporting the welfare of military personnel and their families.

- **Securing the Borders:** Ensuring the security of the borders is essential for preventing illegal immigration and protecting national security. The Trump-Vance border security strategy includes building physical barriers, implementing technological solutions, and enhancing border enforcement.

- **Reforming the Immigration System:** Creating a more efficient and fair legal immigration system is a key priority of the Trump-Vance agenda. Their policies include measures to streamline the immigration process, promote skilled immigration, support family reunification, and address the root causes of illegal immigration.

- **Promoting Diplomatic Solutions:** While maintaining a strong national defense, the Trump-Vance campaign also emphasizes the importance of promoting diplomatic solutions to international conflicts. Their diplomatic strategy includes strengthening alliances, engaging in multilateral diplomacy, promoting trade and economic diplomacy, and supporting conflict resolution and peacebuilding efforts.

Education for the Future

Education reform is a central component of the Trump-Vance vision for America's future. They recognize that access to quality education is essential for promoting social mobility, economic opportunity, and national competitiveness. Their education policies are designed to address disparities in funding and resources, support teachers, and ensure that all students have access to a well-rounded and relevant education.

- **Increasing Funding for Schools:** Addressing funding disparities between school districts and ensuring that all schools receive adequate resources is essential for promoting educational equity. The Trump-Vance education agenda includes measures to increase federal funding for education, support infrastructure improvements, and expand access to early childhood education.

- **Promoting School Choice:** Providing families with a range of educational options is essential for promoting competition, innovation, and improved educational outcomes. The Trump-Vance agenda includes measures to expand charter schools, support voucher programs, and promote homeschooling and alternative education models.

- **Supporting Teachers:** Ensuring that teachers are fairly compensated and have access to professional development opportunities is critical for promoting student achievement. The Trump-Vance education agenda includes measures to increase teacher salaries, enhance professional development, and improve teacher working conditions.

- **Modernizing the Curriculum:** Updating and enhancing the curriculum is essential for preparing students for the demands of the modern economy and society. The Trump-Vance education agenda includes measures to incorporate modern topics and skills, promote STEM education, and support career and technical education.

Healthcare Reform

Healthcare reform is a critical component of the Trump-Vance vision for America's future. Ensuring access to affordable and comprehensive healthcare is essential for promoting social justice and improving health outcomes. Their healthcare policies are designed to expand coverage, reduce costs, and enhance the quality of care.

- **Expanding Healthcare Coverage:** Increasing access to healthcare coverage is essential for ensuring that all Americans have access to the care they need. The Trump-Vance healthcare agenda includes measures to expand Medicaid, support private insurance options, and promote the use of Health Savings Accounts (HSAs).

- **Reducing Healthcare Costs:** Reducing healthcare costs is essential for making healthcare more accessible and affordable. The Trump-Vance healthcare agenda includes measures to promote price transparency, negotiate drug prices, and reduce administrative costs.

- **Enhancing Quality of Care:** Ensuring that healthcare providers use the most effective and up-to-date treatments and interventions is essential for improving health outcomes. The Trump-Vance healthcare agenda includes measures to promote evidence-based practices, improve healthcare delivery, and support healthcare providers.

- **Addressing Health Disparities:** Ensuring that all Americans have access to quality healthcare, regardless of their race, ethnicity, or socioeconomic status, is essential for promoting health equity. The Trump-Vance healthcare agenda includes measures to increase access to care in underserved areas, promote cultural competency, and address the social determinants of health.

The Path Forward

The Trump-Vance partnership represents a bold and innovative vision for America's future. Their comprehensive policy agenda is designed to address the critical issues facing the nation and promote a more prosperous, secure, and inclusive society. By focusing on economic growth, social justice, national security, and educational excellence, they aim to create a brighter and more equitable future for all Americans.

As the Trump-Vance campaign continues to engage with voters and present their policy proposals, it is clear that their vision for the future of the United States is grounded in the principles of fairness, opportunity, and justice. Their commitment to addressing the challenges facing the nation and promoting a more inclusive and prosperous society offers a pathway to a brighter and more hopeful future.

Conclusion

The Trump-Vance partnership represents a dynamic and impactful approach to addressing the critical issues facing the United States. Their comprehensive policy agenda is designed to promote economic growth, social justice, national security, and educational excellence, reflecting a deep commitment to revitalizing the American Dream and ensuring that all Americans have the opportunity to succeed.

By focusing on key areas such as economic reform, social justice, national security, and education, the Trump-Vance campaign aims to create a more vibrant and inclusive society. Their policies are designed to address the root causes of inequality and promote a fair and just society where all individuals have the opportunity to achieve their full potential.

As we look to the future, the Trump-Vance partnership offers a vision of hope, opportunity, and prosperity for all Americans. Their commitment to addressing the challenges facing the nation and promoting a brighter and more inclusive future offers a pathway to a better and more prosperous America.

Join us in supporting the Trump-Vance vision for America's future and help us create a brighter and more hopeful future for all. Together, we can achieve great things and ensure that the American Dream remains alive and well for generations to come.

Other Books by D. E. Sargent:

Restoring America's Greatness through Project 2025

Printed in Dunstable, United Kingdom

70605375R00067